EARTH MYSTERIES
 a beginner's guide

GW00371057

TERESA MOOREY

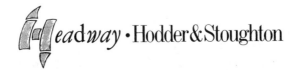

Dedication

For the honey-coloured stone of my beloved Cotswolds

Acknowledgements

Grateful thanks are due to the following for help, advice and access to information: David Elkington, Jay Ellis Ransom, Chel Bardell of the Pan Pacific Pagan Alliance, my friends Jan Morris and John Burford, the Australian Tourist Commission, and very special thanks to Robin Heath, Editor of the *Astrological Association Journal* for providing diagrams in Chapter 3.

A catalogue record for this title is available from the British Library.

ISBN 0 340 70516 7

First published 1998
Impression number 10 9 8 7 6 5 4 3 2 1
Year   2002 2001 2000 1999 1998

Typeset by Transet Limited, Coventry, England.
Printed in Great Britain for Hodder & Stoughton Educational, a division of Hodder Headline plc, 338 Euston Road, London NW1 3BH by Cox and Wyman Limited, Reading, Berks.

CONTENTS

INTRODUCTION

Come forth into the light of things,
Let Nature be your Teacher

Wordsworth, *The Tables Turned*

For some years we have become familiar with pictures of our world taken from space – an emerald against galactic indigo. Rather than fostering a detached perspective, this touching image serves to remind us how beautiful and precious is the planet we inhabit. For many reasons we are beginning to think differently about the earth. No longer do we have to labour, with our hands to the plough, and no longer are we in the developed world dependent upon harvest and hunting to ensure our daily survival; modern methods of food production ensure that supermarket shelves are always full. This may initially have seemed like a liberation, but it is becoming more apparent that it is an estrangement. Most of us live surrounded by concrete, so that we rarely smell the scent of the soil as it opens under fresh rainfall, or muddy our feet, or watch the ever-changing patterns of land and sky.

The drawbacks are twofold. First, it is becoming apparent that our nest is being fouled by the pollutants of modern life and that we are interfering dangerously with the ecosystem. Second, we are experiencing a more subtle but equally fundamental loss. This is a sense of the earth as something more than a provider of basic physical sustenance – it is an awareness of earth as a source of inspiration and spiritual nourishment also, from which we have become separated. Nature has long inspired poetry and mysticism. Now, when we are in danger of losing so much, many people find

1

that the study of our earth is interesting, intriguing, expands knowledge and consciousness, and even inspires worship.

We are beginning to glimpse the fact that those who erected Neolithic structures and stone circles may have possessed a consciousness very different from ours and may have appreciated dimensions, significances and connections that we no longer perceive. Are there mysteries encoded in the landscape? Does the wisdom of our ancestors lie all around us, mutely enshrined in stone remnants? Are there forces beyond the current scientific frontiers with which the earth and ourselves resonate? Is our myth and folklore a secret language of earth power? And is there a magical 'something' in the earth that can lift us out of ourselves into the realm of the mystic, and fill our hearts with worship and wonder? In the following pages we shall be looking at all these questions and providing pointers for further exploration. The field of 'earth mysteries' yields interest and enigma to scientists, anthropologists, historians and archaeologists as well as to those inclined to speculative, mystical, poetical or spiritual approaches. And it can also be, quite simply, intriguing and entertaining. Whatever your orientation, there is something here to captivate.

As earth dances her spiral through space she resonates like a huge gong to galactic radiation at many levels. We do not consciously hear this rhythm, but we are aware of it, subliminally. These low-frequency vibrations – tellingly abbreviated as ELF – are like a great heartbeat that harmonises with our own brainwaves when we are in a state of meditation. Like babes in the womb we are surrounded by our Mother's heartbeat. The earth exerts a profound influence upon our bodies, minds and spirits, and we are more fundamentally a part of her than we may imagine. Her mysteries are our mysteries, her truth is our truth. To begin to understand the subject, perhaps we need to retrieve an ancient understanding of ourselves, the land and the sky as one interdependent whole. In studying the earth we study also ourselves. We may discover fascinating facts that expand scientific understanding, and we are on the trail of the strange, the awesome and the mind enhancing. Who knows where these investigations will lead?

LINES ON THE LANDSCAPE

These lines criss-cross … just like a crystalline structure. You can work them out on any large-scale ordnance map by means of the place-names and standing-stones and earthworks

Dion Fortune, *The Goat-Foot God*

Perhaps the best known and most popular area of earth mysteries' enquiry concerns straight-line formations, more generally known as 'ley lines'. These 'lines on the surface of the earth' are believed to take several forms, and there are many theories about their nature and purpose, ranging from the practical to the mystical and speculative. There is much factual and historical evidence to be evaluated regarding these lines before we consider what they may mean, and we shall be looking at this, in the first instance, before exploring meanings and implications. Interest in ley lines began in the nineteenth century, but the person best known as their exponent – and who coined the term 'ley' – was Alfred Watkins.

Alfred Watkins

Watkins was born in Hereford in 1855. A flour miller by trade, he was also a magistrate and county councillor – a respected and well-known member of the local community. He was interested in archaeology, deeply knowledgeable about the beautiful country in which he lived, and he was a talented and pioneering photographer. In addition, he seems to have possessed a mind that was both open and sharp. On 30 June 1921, Watkins experienced a 'Eureka' moment. His son Allen Watkins described how Alfred happened to look at his map for points of interest, when visiting Backwardine, in Herefordshire.

> *He noticed on the map a straight line that passed over hill tops through various points of interest and these points of interest were all ancient ... suddenly ... His mind was flooded with a rush of images forming one coherent plan ... he saw that over many long years of prehistory, all trackways were in straight lines ... The whole plan of the Old Straight Track stood suddenly revealed ....*

Watkins believed that these tracks were traders' tracks, set down by Neolithic people using basic surveying methods. In fact, ideas about linear formations had been incubating in the nineteenth century, but it fell to Watkins to become the major exponent. His findings were published in his book *The Old Straight Track* in 1925 (see 'Further Reading') and the Straight Track Club was formed in 1926, as a forum for the exchange of ideas and observations. Watkins coined the term 'ley' from the Saxon word meaning a cleared glade. Watkins was not entirely happy about his choice of 'ley', but it seems the term may be more appropriate than he thought. Ley can also be traced back to the Latin *lucere*, to shine, linking with one form of ley-line marker – hills on which beacons were lit at festivals, or as warning of invasion. *Laia* was an English word, used until the seventeenth century to mean 'roadway in a wood', and a Belgian word, *lei* used around Antwerp, referred on old maps to a road going straight to a church.

Watkins' original ideas were expanded by members of the club, and in 1939 Major F. C. Tyler, a leading member, published his book *The*

Geometrical Arrangement of Ancient Sites in which he introduced the notion that the sites were in some fashion sacred. Ley hunting became something of a hobby, and although the Straight Track Club was wound up in 1948, the ideas survived, to be revitalised in the heady hippy era of the 1960s. The Ley Hunters Club was formed by Jimmy Goddard and Philip Heselton in 1962 and a newsletter was started in 1965, called *The Ley Hunter*. This still flourishes as the most well-known and respected UK publication on earth mysteries – indeed, it is the longest running such publication in the world, having an international readership. From that time the entire subject has expanded and acquired many new approaches and dimensions.

Ley markers

It must be understood that the ley system really consists of a series of markers rather than tracks themselves, which have rarely survived in their entirety in England down the centuries, although the same is not true in America, as we shall see. There are a number of features used to mark leys, and some of these occur naturally. To ancient people, living in profound attunement to their environment, it would have been a matter of instinct to choose the land itself as a marker. However, the notion of 'traders' tracks' has now been largely discounted, and more esoteric and mystical interpretations are given for these linear formations – some of which increasingly favour an impulse originating within the earth itself. Here follows the principal ley mark points.

- **Hilltops** – Hilltops are an obvious choice as markers, and Watkins found that all leys had a hilltop marking at least one of their terminals. Not always the highest hill was chosen. A hill of unusual shape might be favoured. Upon many of these hills beacons would have been lit at festivals. The principal ancient festivals occurred at the cross-quarter dates, at the beginning of May, August, November and February, known respectively as Beltane, Lughnasadh, Samhain and Imbolc – we shall be looking at these in more detail in Chapter 4. These were all fire festivals. Later the equinoxes and solstices were also observed as times of celebration.

Sometimes the name of a hill gives an indication of its inclusion in the ley system: for instance, Tan (Welsh for fire as in 'Beltane', meaning fire of the god Bel, the 'shining one'). Cole may be derived from a Welsh term meaning surveyor and Black could refer to he who lit the beacon fires. Red and White might be linked to pottery and salt routes respectively and 'Gold' for the transit of precious metals or related to a ley situated along the path of the Midsummer sunrise. 'Dod' is another name relating to surveyors. In addition, similar names running in a thread, such as Dorrington, Donnington may indicate a ley. It is worth noting in passing that the lighting of a ceremonial fire would have been a ritual, magical act – 'cold-prophet' has been used to mean a wizard or diviner, 'cole' is an obscure Old English word for magician, sorceror or prophet, and the 'man in black' was a name for the high priest who presided at witches' coven meetings. This could be taken as hinting at a sacred and magical meaning to the ley system.

- **Mounds** – There are many varieties of mound, the oldest being the Neolithic long barrow. These unchambered mounds may be up to 100 metres or more in length and perhaps 30 metres in width. Although human remains are usually found at these mounds, we do not know what their precise use might have been. Megalithic tombs contain some form of chamber: these were used for burials, but also for ritual. Indeed, to describe any such structure as a 'burial mound' may be to miss the point, as to identify our churches, with their surrounding graveyards as 'burial sites'. Cairns often date from the Bronze Age and are made of small stones, usually in mountainous districts. You may have noticed when you are climbing up a hill and you can see a cairn above you, there is often a strong impulse to take a stone and add to the pile, as if one were taking part in some instinctive ritual response. Round barrows are prolific in Britain, called 'tump', 'bury', 'castle', 'howe', 'low', 'mount', 'toot' colloquially. Hilltop earthworks, called 'camps' are are also typical markers. All of these may form part of the ley network.
- **Standing stones** – Large, old stones are found all over the British countryside, standing in solitary, brooding majesty. These may often be considered as markstones for the ley system. Some

of these stones have formed the focus of marker sites. Dolmens, quoits and cromlechs are structures of horizontal stone slabs supported by uprights. They are usually assumed to be the remnants of burial mounds, although it is hard to see why the soil around some mounds should have been so totally eroded, while others are completely intact; also there are no half-exposed dolmens. Stone circles such as Avebury, Stonehenge and Castlerigg in the British Isles are also regarded as being sited upon ley lines, and some stones are found in rows, as on Dartmoor, in the South West of England.

- **Churches** – Often built on pagan sites of worship, according to the express command of Pope Gregory in 601CE (Common Era), although some archaeologists dispute this. Some have been built on tumuli or even within stone circles, as Stanton Drew church, in Somerset. Any pre-Reformation church may be a ley-line marker. Some wayside crosses form a similar function, having been formerly standing stones.
- **Other buildings** – Castles, farmsteads and manor houses may also be built on leys.
- **Water** – This is an important element in the ley system, for water reflects light. The reflection of a beacon in a pond would be visible only while standing on the line. Wells, too, form part of leys. Wells were considered holy in ancient times, sacred to the life-giving powers of the Goddess. Fords and moats may also be ley-line indicators.
- **Trees** – These may seem an unlikely marker, because of their temporary nature. However, there may have been a tradition of tree guardians, passed down through the generations of a local family, to keep the clump intact. This possibility is illustrated by the experience of a friend of mine, while attempting to transplant a tree that had seeded itself in her small garden, back into the local wood. Suddenly an old lady appeared 'out of nowhere' and asked her what she was doing. Satisfied that a tree was being planted, not dug up, she disappeared as quickly as she had arrived! Thorn trees are often planted on leys; these are notable for their strange, twisted form and their reputation for being the shape-shifted forms of witches. Trees have many connections

7

with the sacred, and Druids are known to have worshipped in groves. In particular, the Scots Pine, an especially noticeable tree, can be a ley marker. The Scots Pine has mythological connections with dying and resurrecting gods such as Attis and Osiris, who symbolise the seasonal cycle.

- **Roads and tracks** – It is possible that the Romans built their roads on older tracks, and many indigenous people do travel in a straight line. Old tracks may be part of a ley. In particular, crossroads may coincide with a ley, even though the roads converging no longer follow the ancient trackway. Crossroads were considered to be magical places, where witches met, sacred to the Goddess in Her dark aspect. They are loaded with symbolism about life and its choices, the four elements and the four directions – or, in the case of T-junctions, the triple goddess Maiden, Mother and Crone. Hecate was one such, mostly remembered in 'Crone' aspect. (You can find more about the aspects of the Goddess in *Wheel of the Year* – see 'Further Reading'.) Suicides were buried at crossroads, possibly because the sacred nature of the site was subliminally recalled.

- **Notches** – Notches on hills or ridges are also a good indication of leys, providing they are not of modern construction.

- **Cursuses** – Cursuses are parallel banks, with ditches outside, forming an earthen avenue. Constructed in Neolithic times (although once thought to be Roman), cursuses clearly display a straight-line impulse in their builders. Some may be a mile or more in length. Mostly they are linked to burial mounds. There is a cursus nearly two miles long near Stonehenge, and one cursus running to the west of Heathrow airport is also two miles long – much longer than the runways! Aerial photography has been crucial in confirming the presence of such features, and also in identifying other straight formations often indicated only by difference in the colour of the soil, such as tracks on the Yorkshire moors and straight alignments of pits filled with different soils, which have been found in many areas.

Ghost and death roads

Straight roads were constructed to carry the bodies of the dead to cemetaries: examples of these are the medieval Dutch 'Doodwegen' (death roads), Viking 'cult roads; for conducting the bodies of chieftains, and Costa Rican tracks constructed by Native Americans for the same purpose. Reports of these are given in an article 'Lines on the Landscape – Spirit Ways and Death Roads' in *The Ley Hunter*, Issue 126, Spring 1997. The expression 'dead straight' may have a connection with the mode of travel of the spirits of the deceased. The article continues

> ... *old sources referring to the German 'Geisterwegen' (ghost paths) which were thought to run invisibly but straight between cemetaries. Such ghost and death roads probably developed from an archaic core concept. Celtic 'fairy paths' may also relate to this and the ancient Chinese geomantic system of Feng Shui also claimed spirits moved in straight lines.*

However, not all such roads were, in fact, straight: the researcher Ulrich Magin reports that some were explicity not so, in order to prevent the spirits from returning. Here we have a hint that linear formations in general may have a connection with movement of spirits, in some fashion.

Straight Lines in America

Some of the best examples of straight-line features are to be found in the Americas, where the straight tracks themselves are visible.

Northern United States

In the northern United States the Hopewellians, who flourished around 500CE have left imposing earthworks with geometrical layouts and processional avenues. At Marietta, Ohio, a street called 'Sacra Via' preserves an ancient ceremonial path that leads from the Muskingham

river to earthworks that have been carefully maintained. The highly populated sections of the United States are subject to the same problems as the British Isles, in that ancient monuments are all too easily destroyed by the march of urbanisation. However, it is still possible to discern traces of Native American landscape markings that are connected to the ley concept. The more these are hunted out and identified as important, the greater will be the likelihood of their continuing survival.

CALIFORNIA SIERRAS

In the California Sierras the Miwok Indians (now extinct) left trails that were utterly straight, going up and down slopes without any deviation. In the Colorado Desert tracks have been found marked by lines of stone and punctuated by shrines. Straight tracks have been found in Colorado, Arizona and New Mexico. One of the most famous linear features centres around Chaco Canyon, New Mexico, where an ancient people called the Anasazi erected what seems to have been a ritual landscape of chambers (called 'kivas'), Great Houses and a network of extremely straight roads of an amazing extent and exactitude, some running in parallel courses. We cannot be sure what the purpose of these structures may have been, but a scared nature is indicated and it seems the tracks linked points in the landscape rather than communities. Chaco Canyon may have been a centre for ritual and pilgrimage from points throughout the San Juan basin.

SOUTH AMERICA

In **Chile** lines have been found in the Atacama Desert, and aerial photography has revealed similar features in **Bolivia**. Shrines along these have been 'Christianised', in the tradition we have noted in Britain. However, some of the lines are tended and may even still be used for processions and ceremonies. In **Peru** the Nazca lines are notable, and the pampa is covered in straight lines, radiating outwards from points in most cases, like multirayed stars. There are also

figures called 'geoglyphs' where the dark topsoil has been removed, so that a figure is formed by the revealed lighter soil below the surface. One of these is a spider, measuring 46 metres in length. The Inca civilisation left an impressive system of dead straight roads, some of which were reclaimed roads of the pre-Inca peoples. Around Cuzco the formations are most notable: straight lines called 'ceques' connecting scared sites or 'huacas', radiating outwards from a centre and forming a remarkable ceremonial landscape, which may have been a huge terrestrial calender and astronomical system marking the passage of the sun. Unfortunately, this was partly destroyed by the Spaniards. Old straight tracks also survive in **Mexico** in the state of Zacatecas. The Mayan civilisation left evidence of straight roads, and in **Colombia** the still-surviving race of the Kogi, who maintain a living shamanic culture, have a network of straight tracks.

* * *

It seems that when Alfred Watkins had his intuitive glimpse of 'a fairy chain stretched from mountain peak to mountain peak' he grasped something of a significance much vaster than that of his own native land.

The Songlines

I have been told there are no straight-track formations in Australia, according to Chel Bardell, of the Pan Pacific Pagan Alliance.

> … *As to the 'Straight Tracks' – there are two meanings used for these that we know of. If you mean the human-made funeral tracks that were used to carry the dead in a straight line (there being no straight lines in Nature) then no, we don't have any in this country. (The terrain is so rugged there is no way you could form a straight line through most of it!) If you mean Ley Lines as in geophysical energy grids, yes of course we have them – they are world-wide, and I believe the Aborigines were well aware of them. We certainly have 'places of power' such as Uluru (Ayers Rock) that are definite Ley Line points.*

However, I have recently read in *The Ley Hunter*, Issue 128, Autumn 1997, that there are two known stone alignments in Tasmania. These are both found beside the Bay of Fires, about 6 kilometres south south-east of Ansons Bay. Evidence exists close by of camping by Aborigines. The main alignment is 56 metres in length, composed of about 93 flat stones, set almost flush with the surface of the ground. Another stone alignment exists 115 metres to the north, composed of 43 stones and extending 6 metres in a north–south direction. This information is supplied by James Hunter of Tasmina. He continues:

Stone pits and cairns are found on the nearby pebble beach as well as on other coasts on the island. Their function is uncertain but they were certainly constructed by Aboriginal people. Similar stone arrangements were in existence on the west coast in 1830.

We shall be looking further at the idea of leys as an 'energy grid' in Chapter 2. While Australia may not possess the linear examples of the Northern Hemisphere, the Aboriginal Songlines are well known. These seem to be both an expression of the dreaming consciousness of the land and a metaphor for a living landscape, continuously recreating itself. The Songline stories are from a mythical past, but nonetheless possess a reality in the present reminiscent of the Irish tradition of mythical invasions, which seem to depict stages in the creation of the world that are still extant. In Aboriginal belief, at a time in the mythic past great semi-human, semi-divine beings emerged from the earth, or came down from the sky and began wandering over the land. In their travels they left traces of themselves – white quartz may indicate, for instance, the remains of a specific ancestor's torch, a boulder may be his excrement. These ancient paths, or Songlines, are followed by the Aborigines during ceremonial journeys, renewing contact with the land and themselves in the timelessness of the Dreaming. Aboriginal practices are a living example of humans participating in their landscape, drawing life and meaning from it, becoming part of the mystical essence of the earth itself. Earth mysteries' researchers of all types may see much to inspire in this ability!

STATISTICS AND COMPUTERS

It is hard to provide indisputable evidence for the existence of many leys, for some alignments could have occurred by chance. However, some alignments certainly have been proven beyond any doubt. One such example is found in Boscawen-un, Cornwall, and has been studied by the eminent astronomer, Sir Norman Lockyer and the author and ley hunter, John Michell. An aerial view confirms that exact linear positioning of six standing stones, running for three miles from Boscawen-un stone circle. In *The New Ley Hunter's Guide* (see 'Further Reading'), Paul Devereux tells us 'This is such indisputable evidence for leys that a well-known archaeologist was desperate enough to suggest that it was a distortion in the photograph that led to false accuracy! Ley-line theory has long been unpopular with, or merely disregarded by, archaeologists. However, the statistical probability of such lines happening by chance is minuscule.

Computers also have been used in analysis, using data supplied by John Michell on alignments in West Penwith, Cornwall. Fifty-three sites were used, and alignments found by computer. Fifty-three imaginary points were then generated randomly, and the results compared. These supported the premise that alignments had been created deliberately – in the genuine sample a five-point alignment appeared – the chances of this occurring at random would be only once in 250 runs. Five four-point alignments were found where statistically only one would be expected, while the odds against obtaining the 51 three-point alignments that were also obtained are 160 to 1. In *Needles of Stone* (see 'Further Reading'), Tom Graves quotes the actual alignment as being 'of rifle-barrel accuracy'. This study has been criticised on the basis of incomplete data, but there seems little doubt of the statistical case for ley-line formations, and the body of evidence is growing.

Astronomical Alignments

We have mentioned in passing that some leys appear to be astronomically aligned, for instance to the sunrise on Midsummer's Day or other significant festivals. One of the best-known leys is the St Michael's line, running through St Michael's Mount off the Cornish coast, passing through such notable ancient sites as Glastonbury and Avebury and out into the North Sea near Lowestoft. Many churches dedicated to St Michael are built on this ley, and St Michael is linked with the powers of fire and dragon slaying, which may have nothing to do with any defeat of the 'powers of darkness' but may simply refer to the taking on of the dragon-power, or forces from deep inside the earth. On May Day (Beltane) the sun rises along this line and fires lit upon hill-tops would appear as part of the fiery disk if the sun as it came up – so along this line the sun really 'comes to earth'. Here we have a sacred metaphor, linking earth and heavens, on what was to the Celts the first day of summer and an important time ceremonially and actually. Opinions seem to vary regarding this line,

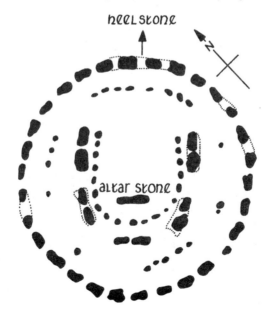

for while many people assume its existence, this has not been proved, and I have also heard it stated categorically that it does not exist! However, there is no doubt that astronomical alignments connected with leys do exist, and they are many and varied. One most notable example of an alignment concerns the Heelstone at Stonehenge, marking the Midsummer sunrise from the centre of the circle, to which the avenue is also aligned. The ancients, more sensitive by far than we are, no doubt resonated to the subtle but far-reaching connections within their environment and marked these by the constructs that still remain today.

Theories about Leys

The existence of leys, or ley lines, in some form, is now probably accepted by just about everyone who is interested in earth mysteries. The idea of some sort of 'energy line' system is also believed implicitly by many. Orthodox opinion, however, has until fairly recently either rejected the linear notion out of hand or simply disregarded it. During this decade there has emerged another theory regarding the meaning of straight-line formations, which is being taken seriously by some sections of the establishment. This theory links archaic (but not 'primitive') forms of human consciousness and worship to the formation of the lines.

The 'ruler' and the Land

The idea that the sovereign obtained his power from the land is an ancient one. A 'Sacred Marriage' which echoed the union of the Goddess and the God, took place in some fashion between the king and the land, which was (and is) the manifestation of the Goddess. Sometimes this was literally enacted in ritual sexual intercourse between the elected ruler and the High Priestess. The sacredness of this bond and its essential nature was undoubted, and without a healthy connection or flow of power between king and country, fertility and growth were missing and nothing could flourish.

This perception is borne out by many myths, most notably that of King Arthur. Arthur tellingly draws the sword from the stone, thus he derives his kingship from the land itself. When he becomes estranged from Guinevere, his queen and personification of land and Goddess, then the land is laid waste and a search is undertaken for the Holy Grail – a feminine symbol – in order to effect healing. Isis, one of the oldest and most complete goddess-forms, is often depicted as crowned with a throne, and her hieroglyph is that of a throne. In crowning ceremonies the monarch is often seated upon a ceremonial stone; to this day British monarchs have been crowned sitting on a medieval chair that holds the Stone of Scone, brought to England from Scotland in 1296 to consolidate the union of the two countries.

Some sources say the king infused the land with his power, which was a divine power, and certainly the tradition of the healing touch of the sovereign is well known. However, it is probably more correct to say that by the grace of the land as Goddess the king stood in lieu of the fertilising God, Her consort, acting as a channel of His power – the God, as the sun, was born, died and was reborn, travelling the cycle, while the Goddess embodied the cycle itself. In this connection some kings were ritually sacrificed. The sun is often taken as a manifestation of the God (although Janet McCrickard in *Eclipse of the Sun* points out that there were many sun goddesses) and it is worthy of note that the sun's rays can be seen vividly coming to earth in a straight line, from between clouds.

An important linguistic element enters into the picture of kingship, in the shape of the Proto-Indo-European root word, 'reg'. This term recurs over and over again in European languages, in connection with morals and social order, kingship and spatial measurement. In French we have *roi* = king, *droit* = right (as directional right and moral right), and *regle* = ruler; in English we have such words as right, direction, region, regal, reign, royal, regime, regular, rectitude; in Latin we have *regere* = to guide straight, *rectitudo* = straightness, *rex* = king, *regimen* = governance; in Spanish we have *real* = royal; in German we have *Reich* = empire, *Regel* = rule, *recht* = right (direction); in Sanskrit we have *raj* = reign. These are to name but a few. Sovereigns were given to moving in processional straight lines and seats of government, from the Hill of Tara in Celtic Ireland to the palace of the Chinese Emperor in the

Forbidden City, were situated in the centre of radiating straight lines. So, in some fashion deeply embedded upon human consciousness, straightness (in all its meanings) kingship and the land seem to be connected. Might this have an importance for ley lines?

Shamanism and Straight Lines

Shamanism is the oldest form of spiritual practice known to humankind. The shamanic outlook assumes that all is alive and that all existence is connected in a cosmic web. Often dismissed as 'primitive' this animistic attitude could be rather considered the highest form of spirituality, as it sees divinity everywhere. The basis of shamanic activity is the practice of 'spirit flight' – a shamanic journey where the consciousness of the shaman leaves her or his body and travels to other dimensions, to effect healing or gain information. The shamanic trance is distinct from forms of mediumship or channelling because it is directed and has a purpose of which the shaman is in control. Shamanism is undergoing a revival at present, and direct experience of the transcendent is sought increasingly in groups and lodges, often with special emphasis upon the North American tradition, which has a living shamanic content. Readers who wish to know more about this can consult *Shamanism – a beginner's guide* in this series.

The desire to enter states of trance seems to be basic to the human condition, and we can see this in its debased form today with our cultural problem with drugs, which numbers of people take recreationally. However, the controlled use of hallucinogens was prevalent in many shamanic cultures and still continues in South America, where peyote and the San Pedro cactus are ingested to induce trance states. When someone enters a state of deep trance, certain images are universally perceived, such as honeycomb, web, tunnel and spiral. (The tunnel with a light at the end of it is commonly seen in near-death experiences.) Following the symbols mentioned, figures evolve, often half-animal, half-human. These 'entoptic' visions are a feature of prehistoric rock art, strongly suggesting that ancient peoples entered trance states, quite possibly induced by drugs, and that certain images are basic to the human nervous system.

The idea of spirit flight seems to be another 'basic' and we find such themes embedded in tradition, myth and folklore: in the earlier section on 'ghost roads' we encountered the belief that the spirits of the dead move in straight lines; witches were said to fly to their meetings on broomsticks, after the application of flying ointment; people often dream of flying – even Father Christmas flies; shamanic cultures worldwide incorporate the notion of spirit journeys as including literal flying, with types of bird a common power animal. Flying is usually in a straight line, hence the term 'as the crow flies'. The final piece of the jigsaw is in place when we make the connection between rulership and shamanism, for the dominance of the tribal shaman evolved into the notion of sacred kingship; in ancient times the shaman was often ruler. The shaman's rod, or wand (or 'talking stick') evolved into the sovereign's sceptre, and is interestingly reminiscent of the surveyor's sighting-rod. This idea, in rather a twisted form, survived into the Tudor era as the 'Divine Right of Kings'. The entire theory linking shamanism with straight-line features is, in fact, borne out by the Kogi tribe, of Columbia, who have straight paths in their land and also have a living, shamanic society, conducting regular out-of body journeys in a tradition of ancient lineage.

So here we have a collection of ideas – straightness, sovereignty and shamanism, spirit flight – that combine to give a historical picture that may rest behind the whole ley system. Paul Devereux, the major exponent of this theory, states in *Shamanism and the Mystery Lines* (see 'Further Reading')

> *'The concept of the straight landscape line originates, I suggest, in a fundamental element of the shamanic experience, indeed in what is arguably the central element of shamanism – magical flight. This is simply a particular version of out-of-body experience … There are not only shamanic traditions, practices, cosmology and rock art – there are shamanic landscapes too. I suggest that this description is more accurate and informative than terms like 'ceremonial landscape' or 'sacred landscape'.*

So straight lines in the landscape, according to this viewpoint, are created by humans as an outward expression of inner experience; images such as that of the White Horse etched upon the hillside at

Uffington, in Oxfordshire, England, and the South American geoglyphs were presumably created so that they are visible in entirety only from the air, thus could be viewed by the shaman as he or she flew over the country. Devereux goes on to say:

> *Landscape lines, leys, alignments are* traces. *They are variously evolved features that had their origins in the ecsomatic experience at the heart of shamanism. They may have become, conceptually, lines of power, then energy; they may have become physical traces, ritual pathways, avenues of the dead or whatever, but they are in essence simply traces of an effect of the human central nervous system transferred to the land. That effect, as we have discussed, is the remarkable ability of the human mind to roam experientially, if not actually beyond the body.*

REACTIONS TO THE SHAMANIC THEORY

The idea that shamanic practice lies behind the creation of leys seems to have found favour with archaeologists. This is not surprising, as shamanism is accepted as having been widely practised among ancient and primitive peoples. Even if the shaman is seen as a capering madman acting out the delusions and superstitions of his tribe, there is no doubt that shamanic beliefs and habits did and do exist, and it seems reasonable that these might have been instrumental in the creation of landscape markers. All this can be accepted without having the slighest understanding of or respect for the spiritual experience concerned. Thus the shamanic theory seems to appeal to archaeologists and aficionados of earth mysteries alike, and is certainly popular and respected.

However, earth mysteries' enthusiasts are themselves separating into two camps: those who apparently favour a scientific, historical and factual approach; those who are more interested in preserving a sense of wonder and worship. To relegate earth phenomena as solely creations of the human mind can be seen to de-soul the whole experience of contact with the earth: nothing is 'really' there in the earth, it is empty and inanimate until our minds impose something upon it. There is no mysterious, sentient universe awaiting our

mystical expansion into it; rather there is empty space waiting for us to fill it. Of course, this can be seen as linked, in a fashion, to the time-honoured Judaeo-Christian tradition of separating spirit from inferior matter, and regarding spirituality as 'rising above'. Many people now regard the mind/matter split as having been largely responsible for the denigration of the material world (N.B. 'mother' and 'matter' come from the same root) and consequently for the plight in which we now find ourselves, in regard to a degraded environment, which has been viewed as there for our exploitation.

Although the 'spirit lines' theory by no means denigrates the earth – and I certainly do not detect that attitude anywhere in the expressions of Paul Devereux – modern paganism seeks rather to expand and develop, to experience mysticism by union with the earthly world, as Goddess, rather than by 'rising above'. The notion that all is a figment of our minds – however important they undoubtedly are – is unattractive in this respect. The term 'unattractive' is applicable, for while we cannot dismiss facts because they do not appeal to us, if something does not enhance one's appreciation of life and sense of worship, one is entitled to call it unattractive. It all depends what you are looking for in a study of earth mysteries: is it important to you to uncover facts or to experience feelings? The latter is the wish of many people, and in this book I attempt to give place to both approaches.

Another possible drawback to the theory could be that spirit 'flight' isn't always literally flying, by any means, but may consist of journeys in Middleworld – i.e. the here-and-now world but enhanced and vitalised by Spirit – or Lowerworld, the 'underground' realm of ancestral entities and deep resources. (Shamanic cosmology traditionally contains three worlds, Upper, Middle and Lower.) While you may indeed fly in any of the 'worlds' you do not have to, and if your power animal (see *Shamanism* in this series) is Wolf or Bear you may find you are going in anything but a straight line! Of course, it is also possible that meandering journeys are also enshrined on the landscape, but that has yet to receive attention as far as I am aware.

Yet another question arises as to why there are apparently no straight formations in Australasia, where there is certainly a shamanic tradition, and one that includes a concept of 'straightness' – for example, where

the departed spirit is linked to the body via a thread, or travels on a rope of air. The extreme ruggedness of the landscape would surely not have prevented some such construction – after all, South America is rugged in places, and the movement of great slabs of stone over many miles with prehistoric technology, as in the creation of Stonehenge, stands evidence to what people will do, if fired by sufficient motive.

These, and other objections may well be soon answered. Certainly, however one reacts to the shamanic theory, there is little doubt that it is the most coherent to emerge regarding ley lines, and the one to have found most favour with the establishment. If this theory is correct, then the 'earth mystery' of ley lines has been solved, leaving us with the mysteries surrounding the cultures that created them, how they thought and worshipped and what their inheritance means for us and our modern concepts. If these are lines of spirit flight it still does not explain to us how we may achieve similar levels of mystical experience. Modern shamanic practitioners might like to experiment with the landscape and see what effect recognition of these 'spirit paths' might have upon states of trance – indeed, I feel sure this has been done already by some.

OUR NEANDERTHAL INHERITANCE?

There remains yet another interesting viewpoint to be examined regarding linear formations: that of possible Neanderthal connection. In his fascinating work *Cities of Dreams* (see 'Further Reading') Stan Gooch makes a convincing and though-provoking case for the theory that a Neanderthal inheritance underlies many of our myths, cultural prejudices and history; that Neanderthal peoples, as distinct from being brutish and ignorant, evolved a society that appears to have been both mystical and complex; that Neanderthal was not totally wiped out, but, in fact, mated with Cro-Magon to bequeath a significant portion of our genetic inheritance!

There are many clues to the importance of Neanderthal, whom Gooch describes as nocturnal, ruled by women and sex and having a large cerebellum, which would have endowed this race with psychic and magical faculties. The worldwide importance of the numbers 7

and 13 can be traced to Neanderthal Moon observance; the fact that myths about the Pleiades star cluster (for instance) are similar in many cultures indicates there was once a worldwide culture that Gooch maintains was far more likely to result from Neanderthal than from extra-terrestrial influence, or Atlanteans (as many authors maintain). Similarly, the equal-armed cross and labyrinth symbol is also found worldwide. In addition, the prevalent fear of spiders and snakes and their links with the nefarious, menstrual taboos, persecutions, hatred and fear of left-handedness also point to Neanderthal derivation, for spiders and snakes are some of the few species where the female is larger than the male.

Attitudes towards all these elements have the characteristic of the repression of the former ruling class by the insurgent lower orders. In other words, if rule by women was overthrown when Cro-Magon overcame Neanderthal, menstruation would be despised (after having been revered by Neanderthal), spiders and snakes demonised as Neanderthal totems, moon worship regarded as potentially evil, etc. There is evidence that Neanderthal was predominantly left-handed. Cro-Magnon wanted the Neanderthal magic, but feared their mystery and their acquaintance with darkness. Neanderthal influence may thus have been passed down to us in witchcraft and other secret traditions, that are regarded with irrational suspicion and are, indeed, hard to define, let alone justify, in a language that is presumably heavily influenced by Cro-Magnon mind-set. Traces of the Neanderthal still persist, Gooch maintains, in certain physical traits – red hair, left-handedness, shape of head, etc. The Australian Aborigines possess many Neanderthal characteristics. Far from being semi-animal, Neanderthal wisdom may be what many of us seek to retrieve.

There is no space here to examine these ideas further. However, in the context of ley lines, Gooch postulates not just a radial network issuing from a central point, but a 'spider's web' of lines where the radials are also connected by a spiral formation. He gives as a notable example a European network, radiating from Alaise, in France and including many related places with similar lines, such as Versailles, Calais, Lausanne, extending to Eleusis on the Nile Delta, Eleusis in Greece and to Kalisz in Poland. All these names may be

derived from the Indo-European root 'ales', 'alis' or 'alles', meaning a meeting point to which people travelled. All the sites are of prehistoric origin, they are all on a system of 28 straight lines down from Alaise and all situated on water of some sort, or a well. Classic Neanderthal, says Gooch, evolved in France. He connects the French formation with other formations worldwide, notably the Nazca lines – and as we have seen, one of the Nazca geoglyphs is a spider. Gooch's idea is of Alaise as a central shrine, with the other points marking shrines where the spiral thread crosses the radials.

> ... are not the radiating lines at Alaise, Cuzco and Nazca really the radial lines of a spider's web? And are not the shrines along them the joins of the connecting spiral thread? And is it not probably further the case that the worshippers went not up and down the straight lines (which would be in any case a little boring) but instead followed the spiral spider path from shrine to shrine across the lines – starting at the outer edge ... working towards the great central shrine ...

> Now, I think, we catch a glimpse of the glory of the spiritual empire of Neanderthal, the mass of people wheeling slowly, night by night, about the central shrine of Alaise ('a meeting place to which people travelled') as the great stars wheeled also above them ...

It is unlikely that these ideas will ever be completely 'proveable' but they certainly 'feel right'. From an earth mysteries, dreamtime perspective, one can just see this happening, feel it as meaningful to a people whose consciousness extended and merged with their surroundings and who understood ritual in their bones. Retrieving this is part of our earth mysteries' quest.

PRACTICE

I am sure that you will like to reflect upon the possible nature of leys – traders' tracks, shamanic pathways, Neanderthal pilgrimage routes – or possibly an energy network, as we shall discuss in Chapter 2. You may like to identify straight formations in your own countryside, walk them and experience them for

yourself. Australian readers may enjoy discovering more about the native Songlines of their country.

As a practical exercise, some readers may like to go out and 'discover' leys for themselves. This is what you will need: sturdy footwear and weatherproof clothing, compass, binoculars, camera (Watkins observed that often the best photographs are obtainable from a position on the ley itself) and an ordnance survey map. Philip Heselton, in *The Elements of Earth Mysteries* recommends a map on the scale 1:50,000. Spread this, first of all, on a table and play around with it, looking for likely ley mark points. You will also need a perspex ruler and a sharp pencil. I have known ley hunters who had a whole wall covered in maps of the local area, with map pins and cotton threads stretched hither and thither over it.

Having located a possible ley, you will need to walk it, as some possible markers may not be on the map, and in any case you will need to get the feel of the land. Remember that a narrow pencil line will be many metres wide, on the land. There is no general agreement about ley width, but Watkins considered that leys were track width. Edge-to-edge alignments is valid in some cases (e.g. for hill forts and stone circles). Heselton recommends chatting to local residents, for sometimes the lore of the locality gives a clue. Look for any unusual feature such as stones concealed in hedges. Naturally, you will need to ask the landowner if you wish to cross private property, and needless to say, always respect the country you are examining. It is sad and surprising that pagans and earth-lovers do not always do this. Detailed instructions for ley hunting are given in *The New Ley Hunter's Guide* by Paul Devereux – see 'Further Reading'.

Ley hunting offers something to most people. It can be a good excuse for a walk and a picnic, some exercise and fresh air; it can be an investigation in sleuthing, history, and geography; it can offer an opportunity to learn more about one's locality and the people who live there, and it can be a pathway to the transcendent and to a sense of oneness with the land, which is then perceived in a fresh light. Take your time. Enjoy your country! Enjoy our world!

EARTh
ENERGIES

Come forth and bring with you a heart
That watches and receives

Wordsworth, *The Tables Turned*

fORCES WIThIN The EARTh

'Energy' is the buzz word of the alternative scene, used to cover all sorts of phenomena and experiences. In particular, it has come to be applied in the earth mysteries field to a subtle force within the earth that is associated with leys, standing stones, ancient monuments and a variety of other places and manifestations. Many people take it as read that there is a network of energy running within the earth and around the globe, and many publications present this as accepted and clearly defined fact, and expand upon it ad lib. Ley lines of myriad types and influences emerge, even

inter-planetary and inter-galactic leys. Leys are linked to health, hauntings, accidents, UFOs, conspiracy theories, Atlanteans …. These ideas are usually fascinating, but sometimes little more than speculation. The 'energies' involved are taken as detectable by dowsing – hence the regular appearance of groups and individuals at sacred sites, clutching rods and pendulums. Some people feel such ideas have gone to extremes.

Recently a more factual and research-based attitude seems to have gained strength, especially among the experienced hard core of earth mysteries' exponents, and a considerable rift seems to be developing between the two camps – the 'energy' camp and the factual camp. The writer Paul Devereux calls this The Great Divide, and there seems to be some ill-feeling deepening this chasm. Scornful remarks are made on the one hand about 'preconceptions and dowsing rods', the 'energy' camp appearing to be regarded as a net-full of deluded fools by those interested principally in research and history, On the other hand, seekers who are 'into' dowsing, theorising and feeling are becoming more stubborn and angry as their pet theories come under assault from the very quarters they looked to for support. It seems important that anyone new to the earth mysteries' field of enquiry should be aware of these different approaches.

Although this rift is regrettable, it is also a graphic and amusing portrait of the age-old rifts between Feeling/Thinking and Intuition/ Sensation, as defined by C. G. Jung, the pioneering psychologist of the early twentieth century. These 'four functions of consciousness' are present in all of us, but individuals generally develop one, two, or maybe three of these consciously, while the other approach/es lie neglected or decried. Feeling, which evaluates in terms of humanity, group bonds, etc. is just as rational a system as Thinking, which evaluates by logic – but these two faculties are often opposed to each other. Intuition is just as valid a perceptual approach – encompassing the totality of a concept and embracing possibilities – as Sensation, which concentrates on the practical details. However, these modes of approach tend to pull in opposite directions. People invariably despise what they do not identify with, or use themselves, failing to see that these are simply different ways of operating, not stupidity, blindness or whatever.

In respect of earth mysteries, Feeling and Intuition seem to have bonded together on one side of the 'Great Divide' versus Thinking and Sensation on the other (although there are many intuitive thinkers in the sphere). Particular individuals will naturally have certain functions more developed than others. Each has their merits and demerits, each is incomplete without the other and each has a significant contribution to make towards the investigation of earth mysteries. Respect and awareness would seem to be vital if there is to be dialogue, support and a moving forwards in human consciousness and wisdom. Tom Graves' succinct remark in *Needles of Stone Revisited* (see 'Further Reading') 'Realities can have value as well as truth', would seem to accord merit to both sides.

ENERGY GRID

The idea of a global network, or energy grid has also come under attack as a superimposition of a modern idea upon the ancient landscape, bringing with it scientific concepts that would have been alien to our forbears, and a type of 'pseudo-spirituality' that merely projects contemporary ideas and knowledge (such as that of electricity) into the environment. However, there are grounds for support of an 'energy grid' in several respects.

- There is no contesting the evidence of dowsers and the feelings of those of us who are sensitive to 'energies'; something is there, although we cannot be exact about what it is.
- I do not see that the concept of a grid, or web, is in the least modern. How ancient is a spider's web? (Remember the Neanderthal!). Concepts of the cosmic web, within which all existence finds connection, is hardly modern. Weaving is an occupation of great antiquity, with ritual and symbolic as well as practical significance – many of the great Mother Goddess Creatrix figures have connections to spiders, and Grandmother Spider appears in North American creation stories. Maybe these concepts, these stories are a reflection of a reality, at some level, contained within the land.
- These 'energies' being often thought of as electrical, or similar, in nature may not be so modern either. Recently, by means of

robotics, a fibre-optic camera has been passed under the door of a sealed chamber in the Great Pyramid to reveal several objects, one of which certainly suggests the ancient Egyptians knew how to make batteries. The consensus of opinion regarding the age of the Great Pyramid seems to be that it is about 3,000 years old. So how new *is* the knowledge of electricity? Perhaps energy grids are an extension of an old creation, not a distorted modern view of the prehistoric. The energy-grid assumption certainly needs to be assessed and reassessed, of course – we must be wary of superimposing our ideas of structure and control on to the landscape – but it is an important concept to many people, which needs to be further researched, but not marginalised or rejected.

The possible nature of earth energies

For centuries, in many different cultures and many different ways, the existence of a type of life force has been postulated. This has been given various names. Hindus call this life energy *prana*. 'Ether' is another term, used to mean a subtle fifth element filling all of space. *Ch'i* is the name given to it by the Chinese and used in their system of environmental balancing called Feng Shui – and it would appear that a similar force within the body is manipulated in the healing treatment of acupuncture. 'Animal magnetism', 'odyle' and 'orgone' are other names given in recent centuries to an energy that appears to occur all over the place, but especially in living creatures. Wilhelm Reich, an ex-pupil of Freud, did many experiments with orgone, which were largely disregarded by the establishment. (Readers wishing to know more about Reich will find him discussed in several of the books recommended in Further Reading, or consult *Wilhelm Reich: Selected Writings*, published by Noonday, USA). The evidence from many different cultures and individuals supports a belief in this force – but what exactly is it?

Several different kinds of force inhabit a dimension that we cannot fully encompass with our present modes of thinking. These 'energies'

inhabit the earth and are sensed by certain people and located by dowsers. However, because this force is intangible results are unreliable and the evidence of dowsers does not always coincide. Ubiquitous use of the word 'energies' is employed to define many different types of force. Like 'psychic' phenomena, so notoriously unreliable in laboratory conditions, the earth spirit continues to prove elusive.

Dowsing

Dowsing has long been accepted as water divining, and the traditional dowsing implement is a hazel rod in the shape of a two-pronged fork, with handle. The two prongs of the rod are held, one in each hand, under tension and the single stem is pointed forwards, in front of the dowser as she or he walks. When there is water underground the rod twitches uncontrollably. Other dowsing implements are pendulums, and dowsing rods which are two L-shaped metal rods easily made from a wire coat-hanger, the shorter ends of which are held in loosely clenched fists, arms at chest height, elbows tucked in, the longer ends of the rods extended in front. Rods swing inwards or outwards and the pendulum circles clockwise or anti-clockwise in response to stimuli. These implements really do move, and apparently quite of their own volition, although some movement may be induced by involuntary muscle spasm on the part of the dowser. Most people can dowse, although some are more proficient than others. Dowsing works because the implement used provides a focus for what is, in fact, sensed unconsciously by the dowser. It is a way of 'tricking' the sixth sense into revealing itself.

However, it is by no means only water that can be found by dowsing. It can be used to locate objects and has actually been accepted into the field of archaeology as a means of finding ancient structures and artefacts before sites are destroyed by bulldozers. Dowsing has become a popular way of investigating earth mysteries, for the rods will move or the pendulum will swing in response to what appears to be earth energies. Ley lines can be dowsed, or confirmed by dowsing, fluctuations in the force field at stone circles, hedges and hill forts,

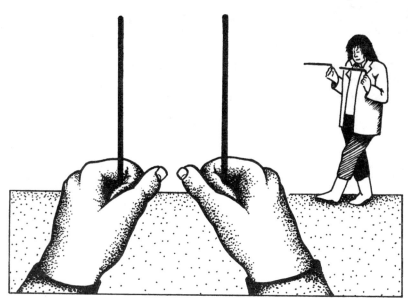

for example, can be dowsed, and 'energy bands' have been detected at different heights on standing stones. The auras of trees can be dowsed, and dowsing is often successfully used to predict the sex of an unborn child. It is possible to dowse the pathway someone has walked, if you give yourself clear instructions to locate it (yet another factor in ley lines). Some specialised and highly skilled dowsers do not even need to visit the site; they simply use a map. Indeed, crimes have even been solved in that manner, with concealed bodies located by the use of a pendulum and a map. From the point of view of earth mysteries' research, this is exciting, but not conclusive, simply because different dowsers do come up with different results and there is insufficient consensus to form a clearly defined picture of earth-energy systems. Also the ability of dowsers varies; just because rods or pendulums move does not mean they are yielding significant information, for this depends on the expertise, experience and concentration of the dowser. Dowsing ability is also influenced by beliefs. Having said this, there are nonetheless many interesting findings and reasonable theories that have been formulated by those working in the field.

LUNAR EFFECTS ON THE EARTH CURRENT

The dowser Tom Graves found that the energy spirals around standing stones fluctuate in accordance with the phase of the moon; zero points in the cycle coincide with the sixth day after new and full moon. The cycles of the moon have for millennia been credited with the power to affect life in many ways, from the growth of plants to the female menstrual cycle. There are more haemorrhages at full moon, greater numbers in admission to psychiatric hospitals, more accidents, and more births. Occultists also use the phases of the moon to harmonise with and lend power to their endeavours – the two most highly charged times in this respect are new and full moon. Astrologers concur with this, for new moon is a time when the energies of sun and moon are working together, while at full moon they are balanced and opposite. Eclipses can occur only at new and full moon. At the quarters (i.e. six days after new and full moons) sun and moon are forming a 90° or square aspect, which can be stressful. Stone Age engravings showing notches in rows of seven confirm that the lunar cycle has been observed and even revered for millennia – hence the importance of the number seven as being the nearest number of whole days to make up a quarter of the lunar cycle (which is approximately 29½ days). This is still reflected in the number of days in our week. The old stones and those who erected them are speaking to us of the significance and hidden meanings in the cosmic rhythms that underpin our lives. What exactly are they saying? Perhaps we need to learn their language before we can understand.

WATER LINES, FAULT LINES AND EARTH LIGHTS

Dowsers working independently of each other confirm that underground water courses tend to intersect beneath many types of

sacred site, from standing stones to churches, which are often built over pagan sites. We know that water is the source of all life and is sensitive to the tidal influence of the moon. The moon has a special resonance with the human body, which is largely water. Water is also considered sacred as a blessing of the Goddess and a transformative element that is both commonplace and unique. Geological fault lines, too, have been found to coincide with the position of standing stones, from research by Paul Devereux and Andrew York. Sacred sites all over the world correspond to areas of fissure and tectonic stress, where there are magnetic and gravitic anomalies and increased mineralisation. Interestingly, all manner of paranormal phenomena, from hauntings to UFO sightings, frequently occur at sacred sites.

The dowser and archaeologist Tom Lethbridge postulated that the earth forces were concentrated at natural features involving water, such as waterfalls, springs and streams, and that such places were able to 'hold' some kind of 'charge' derived from human emotions and energies, the water present possibly acting in the same way as photographic film when it retains an image. These 'charges' are later released, under suitable conditions and in the presence of suitable subjects, to engender experiences of ghosts and ghouls, for example. We shall look further at this idea in a later chapter.

The phenomenon of 'earth lights' has been noted by Paul Devereux. These are light phenomena seemingly produced from the earth itself, especially where there are fault lines. They have properties similar to ball lightning, but are outside the explanation of current scientific knowledge. These lights are familiar to ancient and indigenous peoples. Some Aborigines believe these 'Min min' lights are spirits of ancestors or sorcerors. In the North West of America the Snohomish Indians interpreted the lights as gateways to the Otherworld. The Wintu Indians of California called them 'spirit eaters' and to the Celts they were – and are – fairy lights or corpse candles. These lights have been noted worldwide. In Britain the megalithic complex at Avebury has been known for many such phenomena, among many other places.

Earth lights are of various sizes, sometimes merging and splitting, and they have been known to display what appears to be intelligence,

following people around, dodging and performing acrobatics. The energy involved in these phenomena seems also to have the effect of producing psychic activity, possibly by sensitising persons in close proximity – and the mind of the observer seems also to affect the behaviour of the lights. In *Symbolic Landscapes* (see 'Further Reading') Paul Devereux writes 'I suspect that these lights are nature's most direct intermediary between mind and land'. Are these lights produced by some hidden force within the land, evidence of some form of spirit entity or intelligence? Are they UFOs, as some have suggested? Are they in some fashion chiefly a product of the human mind? Or are they a phenomenon which can be explained in terms of current scientific knowledge, if we uncover more facts?

Crop circles

Large circular shapes formed mysteriously in the corn are well known in the south of England, but they have also been found all over the world including Australasia, and some of these occurrences have been linked to sightings of earth lights. Within the circles the crop is laid down in a circular shape to form a swirled, flattened floor. Sometimes the 'dish' is surrounded by another circle, and sometimes much more complex formations occur. The stems of the crops are usually undamaged and they can be flattened when green, wet, dry, ripe or whatever. There seems to be little consistency concerning the conditions for formation. Some people assert that the 'energies' within these circles are strong, and they have had experience within the circles related to altered states of consciousness, and memorable dreams.

Although some crop circles have been identified as hoaxes, not all can be explained in this way. I have been told that certain indigenous peoples, when asked what they thought was the meaning of crop circles, responded that they were 'the earth screaming'. Could it be that our thoughtless and relentless interference with the land causes energy spirals to spin off and make these circles – and if so, what other, possibly much more damaging manifestations could be brought about in this way? Could it be that by producing the

eternal symbol of the circle in this way, somebody is trying to draw our attention to forces that are beyond our knowledge – to make us stop and think about what we are doing to the ecosystem? If so, she, he or it is not having much success!

The weather

Lore concerning ancient sites includes tales of sudden storms and lightning strikes occurring seemingly as retribution for the violation of the site. In *Needles of Stone Revisited* (see 'Further Reading') Tom Graves postulates that barrows may act as energy stores that absorb the energy involved in potential storms. When the site overloads or is breached by some intrusion, a storm breaks. In Britain, areas where the concentration of barrows, stones, etc. is high are subject to far fewer thunderstorms than other parts of the country, but when storms do occur they are especially ferocious. The Island of Jura, which has the highest number of standing stones, stone circles and the like had little in the way of thunderstorms. It is possible that ancient sites are part of a system of weather control. There are examples of folklore recounting the sudden onset of violent storms when a stone circle or barrow mound is violated.

Power in the stones

Many people have experienced physical effects in relation to standing stones; some dowsers have been flung back and even off their feet by an enormous 'charge'. I have had the interesting experience of being swung from side to side, almost as if I were a pendulum, while touching a certain part of a standing stone in Herefordshire. I could have stopped the movement, but not easily. This was followed by a feeling of giddiness – which I have often experienced at similar sites. Feelings of tingling or warmth are also common – and near where I live in Gloucestershire, near the village of Avening, there is a stone called The Tingle Stone. Other sensations experienced include that of

the stone itself rocking or jumping. Dowsing and generally 'tuning in' to the energy systems at ancient sites and stone circles can be uplifting, but also draining and even potentially damaging to the body, causing headaches, among other reactions.

Tom Graves, in *Needles of Stone* describes dowsable energy patterns around the rim of stone circles, notably the Rollright Stones in Oxfordshire. He also found energy lines leaving the circle at a tangent and travelling across the country, widening to a width of about 2 metres. These he calls 'overgrounds' and he equates them with leys. He gives a picture of a multitude of interconnections between sites, like a telephone exchange. What is being communicated, and why? We cannot answer his until we have a clearer idea of the forces involved. Possibly we require an expansion of our conscious parameters even to understand the 'answer'.

Feng Shui, ch'i and acupuncture

The Chinese system of creating harmony in the environment has recently gained considerable popularity in the Western world. The theory behind Feng Shui is that the proportions and structures in the environment affect the flow of energy – called *ch'i* – resulting in beneficial or adverse effects on human health and general well-being. This working with the environment is called 'geomancy', although the term can also mean divination by casting soil. Interestingly, straight lines are avoided in Feng Shui, for ch'i can move too swiftly along them. The rules of Feng Shui are extremely complex, and indeed some may be based upon the political and financial set-ups in medieval China. However, a Feng Shui practitioner told me that Feng Shui is about common sense and intuition as much as anything: 'Look at a room. How do you think the ch'i will flow? Can it circulate? Does it appear harmonious, balanced, pleasant?' In addition, a Feng Shui consultation can do only so much, for the additional factor of the mind and attitude of the person or persons living in the space will have an effect. If you

wish to know more about the application of Feng Shui, you may like to consult *Feng Shui for Beginners* in this series.

Stagnant, or noxious ch'i is called *sha*. This produces a feeling of oppression, depression, ill-health and other unpleasantness. Sha may be the same as the force behind what dowsers call 'black leys' – lines of adverse influence – and where these are found running through a house, certain dowsers will insert copper wire or crystals to divert the current. This seems to work well, in many cases, but of course the sha or 'black ley' presumably has to go somewhere, and it would seem that a more general sense of respect for our environment and a willingness to learn and adapt might be a more healthy approach. Dabbling with this in an uninformed fashion could be dangerous. It is probable that motorways disrupt leys, or energy flow, because of the speed of the traffic, and electricity pylons are even worse. It has been established that proximity to the National Grid causes ill-health, although this has not been officially linked to ley-line concepts because the existence of leys has not been confirmed to the satisfaction of the scientific community.

Ch'i also flows in the human body along 'meridians'; it is along these meridians that the acupuncture points are found. When needles are inserted at these places, the energy flow is affected – similarly, massage of these points can help and a technique called 'moxibustion' where incense is burnt at the acupuncture points can also form part of the therapy. Parallels between the living body of the earth and the human body do suggest themselves and are becoming more acceptable, especially since the 'Gaia hypothesis' was formulated by J.E. Lovelock: we shall be covering this in a later chapter. In *Needles of Stone* Tom Graves postulates that standing stones may be the earth equivalent of acupuncture. By the same token, beacon fires would equate with moxibustion, and perhaps dancing and similar folk ritual would be the equivalent of massaging the earth! Megalithic peoples in Britain may have used a combined system of Feng Shui and 'earth acupuncture'. Graves tells us

> *In a system of earth acupuncture, there could hardly be a more obvious 'needle' than a standing stone … British geomancy, if it did exist, would seem to have been a system of earth acupuncture, with the sacred sites as acupuncture points in energy channels*

*both sinuous and straight, and with standing stones and the like
as massive needles of stone. And if that is the case, we now need
to look again at those stones, with a rather different point of view:
to put them to use, in the present rather than the past.*

Janet and Colin Bord, in *The Secret Country* (see 'Further Reading')
also suggest that it is possible that rerouting of power by means of
standing stones has caused a depletion in earth energies, and that,
in fact, this was a destructive or manipulative act on the part of
megalithic cultures. Climate and fertility of the land declined over
large, upland areas of Britain towards the end of the Bronze Age,
and this could have been because the energy store of the earth had
depleted. The folk memory of this may be contained in tales of
magic cows that were milked dry, such as the White Cow of
Mitchell's Ford in Shropshire, the White Cow of Callanish, the Dun
Cow of Warwick, and others. We have encountered the connection
between the root word 'reg' and straightness and sovereignty. This
equates with control. In the Stone Age, people may have lived in
conscious harmony in a matrifocal society, but this gave way to the
conscious control of patriarchal attitudes that came later. The
shaman who participated in the spirit world gave way to the king
with his sceptre. Living with the earth gave way to controlling her:
straight lines, kingship, rectitude, control. If this happened it may
not have been a good thing. Chinese wisdom discourages straight
lines. However, there *are* straight lines in nature – sunbeams coming
to earth through a cloud are straight, the stems of some plants are
straight. Perhaps there is a place both for the straight and the
sinuous, in different contexts.

MAGIC

Magic is best defined as 'the art of causing changes in consciousness
at will'. However, there is more to magic than changing ourselves
(although that is arguably the greatest magic of all) for if we truly
and radically alter something in our personal 'field' inevitably we
alter our environment. Ritual helps us to change our consciousness,
and the raising of power, effected in various ways by witches and

magicians provides the force behind our endeavours. The 'power' is assumed to come from the subtle energy centres in the human body – also called chakras – and it can be raised by dancing, chanting or other means. Power raised by a ritual dance rises in a cone shape and can be directed by the practitioner. Magical rites are conducted within a 'magic circle' created by visualisation and ritual; this circle provides both a protection against stray forces that may be attracted to the workings and also a means of containment for the force raised until it is time for release. Of course, the whole idea of magic is often scoffed at, but it is real and it works, although not always simply or easily. Witchcraft is called 'the Old Religion' because it is much more than a few spells, being a tradition of Goddess worship and profound identification with the land. It is assumed to have been handed down from Neolithic, if not Palaeolithic times – indeed we may even have the Neanderthal to thank! If you wish to find out more about this subject you may like to read *Witchcraft – a beginner's guide* in this series.

Analogies between the force raised in magic and the forces we have been postulating within the earth and concentrated at ancient sites are obvious, and indeed the experience of them is similar – although the energies present in one's own magic circle are more familiar and predictable, in a sense. The energies 'out there' connect with one's own personal field – they can be powerful, 'moving' in several senses, scary and sublime. Stone circles seem to echo the occultists's magic circle, and indeed there is often a feeling of timelessness, stillness and containment within them. I have experienced this especially strongly at the stone circle at Castlerigg, set within its cauldron of hills. Stone circles lend themselves to magical and ritual working, although care needs to be taken in this respect: this energy is not for messing around with. Some sites, notably the Rollright Stones in Oxfordshire, have been desecrated by disgusting rites involving living sacrifice of animals, leaving the unpleasant psychic field that one might expect. True witches, nature lovers and students of the occult are not involved in such practices, for the rule is always 'harm none'. However, there will always be some people who enjoy being shocking; the chances are that they will sooner or later receive a substantial 'shock' themselves!

So it is possible that stone circles, standing stones and the like are part of an ancient magical system, used to enhance crop yield and animal and human fertility. Defence may also have been a factor. The dowser Colin Pope has detected a 'psychic force field' around the hill fort at Crickley Hill in Gloucestershire, which has a 'gate' that would have been known only to initiates. It is possible that such a force field could be intensified by ritual to the point where invaders were filled with a sense of discouragement or even of terror at these places; they may have 'seen' guardian thought forms, created by the 'mind stuff' of the practitioners and marshalled to defend the locality. Such guardians have been seen at barrow mounds and sacred sites as black and frightening shapes, or sensed as a feeling of fear. It has been suggested that these entities also guard the pyramids (hence the curse of Tutankhamen), having been created and invested with strength by cruel and highly effective rituals on the part of the Egyptians.

More subtle explanations may lie behind the structures, such as a focus for psychic forces. Achievement of altered states of consciousness, telepathy over vast areas, psychokinesis and other faculties would be enhanced at these sites. Prophecy, spirit flight, clairvoyance and other forms of psychic faculties are possessed by many, if not all, humans and, if Stan Gooch is right, Neanderthal with his enhanced cerebellum was *much* more receptive to these forces than modern humans.

Morphogenetic fields

The existence of other levels of reality is to some extent supported by the work of the biologist Rupert Sheldrake. In his *Hypothesis of Formative Causation* Sheldrake put forward the notion of a non-physical pattern behind physical form. His 'morphogenetic fields' are fields of information, located outside of the individual brain and thus giving access by an individual to the memory of the species, by a process of 'morphic resonance'. This would explain how a seed can become a plant, or an egg a chicken (or a fertilised ovum a human),

and would explain why discoveries are made almost simultaneously around the world, by people who have no identifiable connection: it seems that once something has been done, or thought for the first time it is easier for others to do it or think it, because some subtle pathway has been opened. Morphogenetic fields are thought to be more readily accessed by certain people, notably the young (who are reputed to be more open to experiencing 'ghosts', 'spirit companions', and such like). The scientific description of this phenomenon is 'species memory' but it exhibits sound characteristics identical to all the esoteric ideas about telepathy, cosmic web, etc. Thus, morphogenetic fields may be linked in some way to our study of earth mysteries and the 'energies' in leys, stone circles, and the like. It is reasonable to assume that the ancients were more in tune with their environment and with other levels of existence than we are, so they may have experienced greater 'morphic resonance'.

The findings of science

Dowsing and other methods of experiencing and defining what happens at ancient sites have their limits. In an effort to provide more substantial evidence, the Dragon Project – named after the Chinese representation of earth energies – was formed in 1977. This was an interdisciplinary research programme involving electrical engineers, dowsers, physicists, psychologists, artists, psychometrists, scientists and other workers in the area. Its objectives were 'To detect by quantifiable physical and biological means, the manifestation of "earth energies" at prehistoric sites and to relate this to the ultimate nature of earth energy and to the suspected prehistoric manipulation of this energy.'

The project centred on the Rollright Stones, in Oxfordshire, as being a readily accessible site. Funds were in short supply and this hampered the work. The Project recognised that it might be dealing with unknown energies but started by monitoring those known to science. Here are the findings in brief, condensed from the account given by Philip Heselton in *Elements of Earth Mysteries* (see Further Reading).

Ultrasound An ultrasonic pulsing at two-second intervals was recorded at the outlying 'King Stone' at dawn, in autumn of 1978. Later that year there was an occasion when the normal background level of ultrasound was absent within the stone circle. In February 1979 just before sunrise at new moon and about half an hour before sunrise at full moon there was an outburst of ultrasonic pulsing, continuing through sunrise and for up to two to three hours beyond it. This lessened through the spring and was gone in the summer. No overall pattern of ultrasonics has been established.

Radiation Radiation exists naturally, emanating from rocks in the earth's crust, and can be monitored by a Geiger counter. Granite rock is especially radioactive and increased natural radiation has been shown to produce transitory but vivid changes of consciousness in some individuals. Radiation anomalies tend to occur at many sites: some have a lower level of background radiation than their surroundings and some have a higher level. There are records of much greater variations of readings at stone circles than at control sites, but again no pattern has been defined.

Magnetism There is a magnetic field within the Rollright circle that fluctuates relative to the outside surroundings over a period of hours. Two stones on the west side of the circle have been found to pulse magnetically. An experiment with tubes of brine shrimp, which are sensitive to magnetic fields, showed that they seemed to group at the end of the tube which was nearest the stones.

Photography Discharges have been revealed from the top of one stone in the Rollright circle, and an infra-red photograph of the King Stone showed a glow about the stone and a ray shooting off at an angle, which has not been explained.

Radio In certain places around (but not within) the circle electronic signals could be picked up at ground level. No explanation for this has been forthcoming.

Investigative work is still continuing in many other sites, but funds are always in short supply. While nothing definite has been found, enough has been uncovered to suggest that something is going on at these places and to invite further research. In 1987 the Dragon

Project Trust was set up to continue the work and to study the effects on human consciousness at sites where anomalous phenomena have been recorded. Heselton writes: 'The Trust is the only organization attempting research into measurable or observable energy effects at ancient sites and, without funds, the Project will die. Donations of money, work and skills will be gratefully received by the Trust, c/o Empress, PO Box 92, Penzance, Cornwall TR18 2XL.'

The pulse of the earth

There seems little doubt that there are rhythms within the earth that may affect out lives intimately, though intangibly. It is written that things have not only to be seen to be believed but have to be believed to be seen! One of the objectives of earth mysteries' research is to enable us to gain a greater scientific and quantifiable understanding of the earth. Another approach is to allow ourselves to 'tune in' in more subtle ways, with the body of the earth and to respond to her pulses. By allowing ourselves to adopt an open and passive approach, the earth can communicate with us, through our five senses and perhaps through what is generally termed our 'sixth sense'. However, we may be able to make ourselves 'actively' open, through dowsing.

PRACTICE – DOWSING

Anyone can dowse, but if you wish to learn to do it properly and effectively, train with an experienced dowser. Alternative shops and centres often have advertisements, and some of these will doubtless provide contacts in the earth mysteries' field. You can also contact *The Ley Hunter* magazine (address in Further Reading) or the British Society of Dowsers, Sycamore Cottage, Tamley Lane, Hastingleigh, Ashford, Kent TN25 5H. Of course, you can also teach yourself, and a good book to start with is *Dowsing for Beginners* by Naomi Ozaniec, in this series.

I dowse for the feeling that I get from it, a sensation that I can only describe as 'merging'. This tends to be joyful, poetical and even revelational, and such sensations can 'set me up' for hours, or even days, giving me increased energy and expanded consciousness. I feel able to complete a connection between me and the land. However, not everyone experiences these feelings; many people dowse to obtain specific information.

Practice and the ability to cultivate a certain detachment are vital when dowsing, because the rods or pendulum may respond to one's beliefs, rather than to something more objective. It is important to be clear about what you are seeking. Usually the pendulum is 'programmed' by the dowser, clearly defining that clockwise means 'yes', anticlockwise 'no', for instance. You can do this by asking yes–no questions to which you know the answer and noting the result, thus a connection is being forged between your unconscious mind and the pendulum.

A pendulum is a weight of some sort attached to a piece of string – many people like to use a crystal dangled from a length of chain. Experiment with what works best for you. Relax, support your arm and dangle the pendulum over the area or object that you are dowsing. If the pendulum does not move this time, don't worry. Don't try for too long at a time: put the pendulum away and try another day. There is no reason why it should not work for you. I find the pendulum moves 'on its own', but experienced dowsers usually set it swinging and then let it find its own direction. I saw the dowser Colin Pope do this effectively at the start of a recent field trip, to discover how many people were going to arrive. He swung the pendulum and counted. When he got to sixteen the pendulum hesitated and began to move back and forth. This was repeated a couple of times. Sixteen people did indeed arrive over the next ten minutes.

I find dowsing rods easier to use than a pendulum. These can be obtained in 'New Age' shops, but it is cheaper to make your own from a wire coat-hanger. Make two rods (although you can dowse with one) bent at a right angle, the side you hold should

be 12 cm long, the other side should be 27 cm in length, and this projects in front of you. Hold the short sides loosely in your fists at chest level, arms bent at your sides (see illustration on page 30). Tell yourself what you are dowsing; it could be the aura or energy field of a tree (all living things have an aura and these can be seen by sensitive people, or sensed – even some inanimate objects have auras of a type). Approach the tree slowly from several metres away and watch to see when the rods swing – they may swing outwards or inwards. This practice can make you feel close to the essence of the tree, which can be beautiful. When you are experienced you may be able to tell whether the tree is in good health or not by the shape and extent of its aura. I have seen a tree's aura extended by an attitude of welcome and gentleness.

Practise your dowsing carefully. It is possible to get overloaded, depleted and confused by too much exposure and you need to monitor your reactions and feelings carefully, or you could make yourself ill. I find that if it becomes 'too much' it is a good idea to move away from the site, put down rods or pendulum and kneel or sit, palms flat on the earth, visualising any energy that may be harmful, draining away into the great body of the earth. Breathe evenly and centre yourself. If you are dowsing for 'energy patterns' at sacred sites, leys, etc, make a note of your findings, but keep an open mind regarding what they may mean.

3
SACRED SITE AND STRUCTURE

When Man learns to create with the same vision with which the divine powers have created Nature and made physical things, then will the temple be built on Earth

Rudolph Steiner

Ḋoly connections

Many of the reasons for the creation of barrows and stone circles remain a mystery. They were constructed by a people with a different outlook from ours, a people whose mystical attunement to

the earth no doubt gave them a special relationship with her. Earth was Goddess, embodiment of the Creatrix, and as such holy. All that manifests partook of the sacred. Human bodies, made from the minerals of the earth, were returned to the earth in a tomb that was also womb, that would in some fashion rebirth them. In *The Ancient British Goddess* (see Further Reading) Kathy Jones writes 'For the long ages of the Palaeolithic Era the Goddess reigned alone ... the Earth was Her body ... The people of those times knew about the natural rhythms of Mother Earth ... They knew how to correctly position stones and mounds in order to maintain the balance and harmony of their Mother's Body.' It is widely accepted that peaceful worship of the Ancient Great Mother existed almost universally in the Stone Ages, and while there is no incontestable proof of this, to enter the 'aura' of this belief, to clothe oneself in the sense of mystical union with the natural world is akin to walking through a doorway to a different room in the mind. From this 'room' we may look out upon the world with the eyes of our ancestors and we see that their vision was not primitive, but a thing of beauty and a participation in a mystery. This sense may come upon us especially at ancient 'sacred sites'.

The cycle of the seasons, sexuality and fertility of human, animal and plant were also held sacred, and many barrow mounds celebrate the 'mating' of earth and sky. For instance, the barrow at Stoney Littleton in the English Cotswolds is shaped so that every year, for a few moments on Midwinter's Day, and the day or two on either side of it, the bright fingers of the sun's rays penetrate right through to the end of the long passage at the centre of the mound, illuminating a natural cup mark on a special stone. The shape of this passage is reminiscent of the vagina, and a 'cup' is a natural symbol of the female womb, thus the fertilising aspect of the sun is suggested. This alignment is to some extent a 'mystery' for it does not fully answer the 'why' and the 'how' of our remote ancestors' building activities. The experience of being there, at the special moment when earth and sky unite, when the interior of the stone glows in response to the presence of the sun, is awesome. The earth sings and exudes joyful response that spirals and shimmers upwards, visible to 'inner sight' and energising the environment.

There are many such alignments – New Grange, in Northern Ireland, is another famous example.

It is not hard to see why our forbears should have marked the wonderment of the sun's yearly return in this way. However, the way the Megalithic peoples interpreted the cycles of moon and sun was quite complex, and to understand this we need to turn to the basics of numbers and geometry.

God is a geometer

Kepler, the great astronomer, is believed to have said 'Geometry is God Himself' and since ancient times numbers have been regarded as encoding secrets and enshrining esoteric truth. Pythagoras is known to have formulated important laws of number, but he merely restated knowledge that was far more ancient. As well as expressing quantity, numbers also conveyed quality. Unity and duality are not hard to grasp, but meanings were attached to all numbers, and especially to those with single figures. Seven, for instance, was a number of mystery and 'inwardness'; three had connotations of play, creativity and harmony, and so on. Numbers also expressed rhythm, harmony, cosmic law, and they were found to underpin creation. Numbers relate to music. Pythagoras found that a string, when stretched, sounds a note that harmonises with other strings when their lengths are numerically related; Goethe referred to the geometry of sacred architecture as 'frozen music'. Geometry lies behind the structure of a flower, the proportions of the human body and the intertwined dance of the sun/moon/earth, and this fact was noted and expressed by Megalithic peoples who found it so important that they invested stupendous effort in constructing great circles of stone as markers.

A most interesting series of numbers is the Fibonacci series, so called after the pre-Renaissance mathematician, who was their exponent, but probably not their originator. Starting from Nothing – 0 – we go to Something – 1. A creation metaphor? From then each new number is formed by adding together the two previous numbers forming the series 0 1 1 2 3 5 8 13 21 34 55 89 …. This pattern is

found all over the natural world, for example in the growth of plants, the mating cycles of insects and animals, even in the hydrogen atom. The further along this series one travels, the nearer adjacent numbers approach to the proportion phi (Φ), called the Golden Section.

The Golden Section

Simply, we can define it this way. The Golden Section refers to the division of a line, or rectangle, in such a way that the smaller section is to the larger section as the larger section is to the whole. Tests have shown that to most people this is the most natural and visually pleasing place to make a division. The Golden Section is not difficult to express as a proportion but as a decimal it is literally the most irrational of numbers because it does not reveal a pattern. It is expressed as 1.618033989 ....

The phi proportion is found in sacred structures from the pyramids to the Parthenon, to Gothic cathedrals, and in stone circles. Although myriad interrelationships may be discovered, sacred geometry is not complex in essence; all it needs is a straightedge and a compass, for it is not to do with quantitative measurement, but with ratio and proportion. From the basic geometry of a square, using the said compass and straightedge, a Golden Rectangle can be generated, from which can be derived, by similar means the shape of a pentagon (Fig. 3.1), and thence a pentagram, or five-point star (Fig. 3.2). The relationship between the side of a pentagon and the 'arm' of the pentagram drawn within it is phi.

The pentagram is an occult symbol of the same proportions as the human body, and is often taken to signify the female body (Fig. 3.3). It is also symbolic of the five elements, Earth, Fire, Air, Water and Ether. Derived from the square, which signifies the earth (the number four – four points, four sides to a square – is the number of the material world), the pentagram conveys the numinosity of the earthly sphere. Pentagram shapes are found throughout nature, notably in the five-fold petals of some flowers.

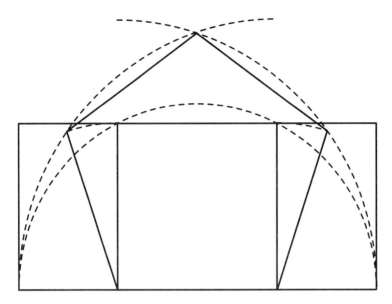

Figure 3.1 The Golden Section

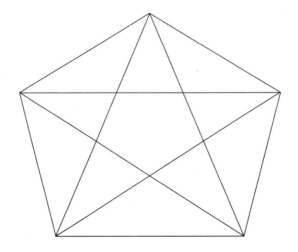

Figure 3.2 The pentagram

Figure 3.3

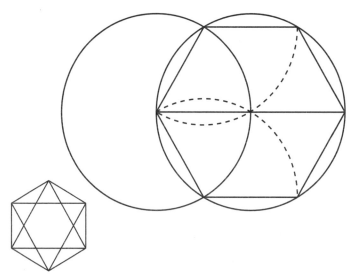

Figure 3.4 Constructing a hexagram

The hexagram, or six-point star, is symbolic of the male body, or the union of male and female represented in the interlocking triangles (Fig. 3.4). It is simply derived from the *Vesica Piscis* which consists of two interlocking circles (the circle is the symbol for the heavens), whose circumferences each pass through the centre of the other,

forming a vulva shape and taken as a symbol of the Goddess. The Vesica Piscis is found on the lid of the Chalice Well at Glastonbury in the west of England (Fig. 3.5), which is believed to be a site of great antiquity, dedicated to the Goddess and later Christianised. The shape of the Vesica also underlies the construction of Castlerigg stone circle in Northumbria, a circle which also encodes many movements of the sun and moon.

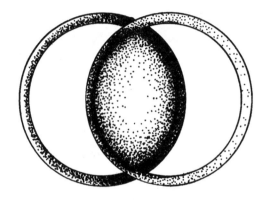

Figure 3.5

Stonehenge and the Lunation Triangle

The great stone circle of Stonehenge, situated on Salisbury Plain in the south-west of England, has been called the Giant's Dance, in a reference to the supposed 'supernatural' placement of the huge stone slabs. But the 'dance' may also refer to the primordial 'dance' or earth, moon and sun. Robin Heath suggests that Stonehenge may be a representation of planet earth, for the long sides of the Station Stone rectangle that lies within Stonehenge (Fig. 3.6a) reflect the position of the Tropics of Cancer and Capricorn (Fig. 3.6b). We will look at this in more detail later in this chapter.

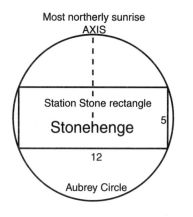

Figure 3.6a

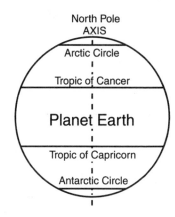

Figure 3.6b

First we need to consider some basic astronomy and to come back to the notion that 'God is a geometer' (and if He is a geometer, then perhaps the Goddess Herself is the geometry?). Our Gregorian calendar and our folklore imply a dilemma between the numbers 12 and 13 in respect of dividing the year. This has to do with the number of lunar cycles in a year, and there are two major cycles to consider:

- **Sidereal cycle** (cycle by the stars) It takes 27.322 days for the moon to move from the start of Aries, say, around the zodiac and back again, to the start of Aries. The moon makes 13 rounds of the zodiac in 355 days, thus there are 13 sidereal 'months' (the word 'month' is derived from 'moon').
- **Lunation month** This is the passage from one full moon to the next, which is determined by the relative positions of the sun and moon in respect of earth. The time span for this is 29.53 days. Most years have 13 full *or* new moons, but never both, and some years include only 12 of each – so there are 12 full 'lunation months'. In addition, there is an 'eclipse year' of 346 days. In an easy system of eclipse prediction, with the aid of simple geometry encoded in Stonehenge, and a cord – believed to have been used by the Druids – the year is implicitly divided into 12.

Here we have a 12/13 dilemma that nestles within folklore and tradition. For while 13 is considered 'unlucky for some' it is also magical (13 is the traditional number for a witches' coven). It is also one of the Fibonacci series – 12 is not. The numbers 12 and 13 occur in many stories: Arthur plus his 12 Knights = 13, Christ with his 12 disciples = 13, and this theme recurs across the Atlantic in Mayan myth. Here the thirteenth is both a sacrifice and a redeemer. In tales such as 'Sleeping Beauty' it is the thirteenth fairy who lays a curse upon the beautiful princess. Neanderthal, whom we encountered earlier, may have been nocturnal and moon worshipping, valuing the number 13, and this would have been reason enough for rejecting it by descendants who feared (yet desired) Neanderthal secrets, and found the easily divisible 'round number' 12 more rational.

The Lunation Triangle

The numbers 12 and 13 may be considered 'solar' and 'lunar' numbers respectively. Here we have a striking geometric occurrence. Take a Pythagorean triangle with sides 13:12:5 (Fig. 3.7). Divide the '5' side into 2 and 3 (Fibonacci numbers) and draw an 'intermediate hypotenuse' from this new point to the apex. The length of this intermediate hypotenuse is 12.369. In fact, 12.368 is the exact

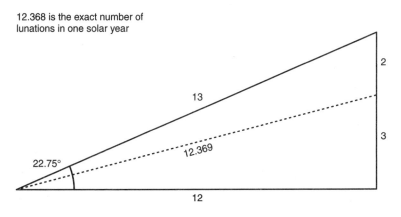

12.368 is the exact number of lunations in one solar year

Figure 3.7 The Lunation Triangle

number of lunations (i.e. cycles from full moon to full moon) in a year – hence a 'sacred marriage' of moon and sun is made within the triangle – and the apex angle reflects the axial tilt of the earth, which averages 22.75 degrees. The Station Stone rectangle in Stonehenge is comprised of two such triangles. Furthermore, if a pentagram is drawn within a circle of radius 13 units (e.g. the Aubrey circle, within which the Station Stone rectangle is constructed (Fig. 3.8a)) each of its star arms will measure 12.364 units (Fig. 3.8b) – close to the number of lunations in a year. Furthermore, the five star arms add up to 61.82 units which is 100 × phi' (phi' is the reciprocal of phi, or 1/phi). There is no denying the stunning geometric implications of the sun/moon relationship, permeated with phi, related to an ancient magical symbol and encoded in Stonehenge. In addition, the density of the earth is almost phi times that of the moon, and the circles of Stonehenge, when viewed from high overhead at the polar axis, appear as Golden Ellipses (i.e. ellipses where the major: minor axes are in the ratio of phi).

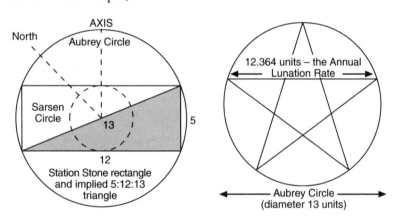

Figure 3.8a   Figure 3.8b

Triangles placed adjacent to the Lunation Triangle and given the same treatment as the Lunation Triangle, having an intermediate hypotenuse drawn to the 3:2 point on the shortest side, also reveal lunar secrets. The 13:14 triangle has an intermediate hypotenuse of 13:369 – the number of lunar orbits (i.e. sidereal months) in a year

The intermediate hypotenuse yields the number of
times the Moon passes a fixed star in one year

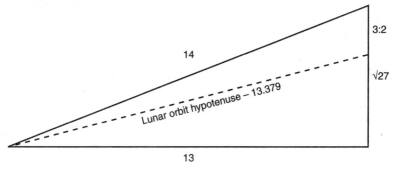

Figure 3.9 Sidereal lunar month triangle

The intermediate hypotenuse yields a length which in comparison
to the 12 side forms the ratio of eclipse year to solar year

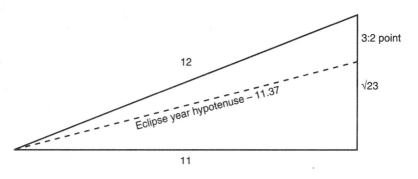

Figure 3.10 The eclipse year triangle

is 13.368. The 12:11 triangle treated in the same way yields 11.37;
11.37 scaled to the 12 months of the year is the same as 346 scaled
to 365.242 (i.e. the eclipse year and the solar year. This is also basic
geometry, which may seem conceptual, until we render it as a
drawing, and notice that it forms part of the familiar shape of the
snail's shell. As Robin Heath comments in 'The Sacred Marriage
Part 2' from the *Astrological Association Journal*, July/August 1995:

*The home of the humble snail is an exquisite phi-based spiral,
and here we are witnessing a similar shape evolving from Sun,
Moon Earth cycles. Countless billions of gastropods will be happy
to discover that they evolved their mobile homes to a cosmic beat,
all shot through with phi. It's worth remembering at this point
that Stonehenge is built on chalk – the remnants of countless
trillions of such shells ...*

Chalk has been described as the most favourable rock for psychic
experiences or rituals. Here we have encountered so many
associations that it is almost bewildering, encapsulated in the saying
'As above, so below' and returning us to that catch-all word 'holistic'.

MORE LEY LINES?

Before we leave Stonehenge there is yet another amazing fact, to
which Robin Heath draws our attention in 'The Lunation Triangle'
Issue 127 of *The Ley Hunter* magazine. There has long been
speculation as to why Bluestones from the Preseli mountains were
so important in the construction of Stonehenge. Robin reveals the
Preseli site is part of yet another enormous Lunation Triangle, with
the 13 side formed by a line from the Gors Fawr stone ellipse just
below the Bluestone quarry, the 12 side from Stonehenge to Lundy
Island, and the 3:2 point on the short 5 side, between Lundy and
Gors Fawr marked by Caldey Island. The implications of these facts
and ideas are truly far reaching, not only in terms of the knowledge
and technical ability of Megalithic people, but in terms of the
interconnections of so many aspects of creation. I think we sense
these interconnections at barrows, stone circles and the like. There
is a 'presence' there – vast, awesome and inspiring.

* * *

This section and the preceding three have formed a 'taster' only.
If you wish to know more please consult the following articles
and books by Robin Heath: 'The Lunation Triangle', Issue 127,
The Ley Hunter; 'The Sacred Marriage', *Astrological Association
Journal*, Vol. 37, No 4; *A Key To Stonehenge*, Bluestone Press 1993;

Sun, Moon, Man, Woman – a New Look at the Ancient Mysteries, no longer available, but copies exist in VT Library and elsewhere. A good basic source for sacred geometry is the chapter of that name (Chapter Five) of Paul Devereux, *Earth Memory* – please see Further Reading.

Architecture

Geometric patterns have been incorporated into many structures. The Pyramids are an obvious example. The Pyramids possess solar and stellar alignments and are related in many ways to the proportions of the earth. The pyramid shape has been shown to possess enigmatic qualities and powers, not only to change the moods and health of people within a pyramid structure, but also to preserve organic matter and sharpen razor blades. Ancient secrets from pagan temple building were handed down and incorporated into the building of churches and cathedrals. The Knights Templar were supposed, ostensibly, to guard pilgrims but their true activities seem to have been of a far more esoteric bent, causing them to be persecuted and destroyed by the Church at a later date. They brought back from the Middle East secrets and traditions that were also employed in church design, and the first Gothic buildings appeared shortly after the return of the original Knights in the twelfth century. The cathedral at Chartres in France is a famous illustration, housing a whole train of examples of sacred geometry, notably the pentagram. Glastonbury Abbey is another case, based on the Vesica Piscis. The majesty of Gothic architecture breathes an arcane power. It is probable that it affects sound and the impact of sound on the human psyche, among other things. Secrets were no doubt protected by the masons, who incorporated in church architecture many figures that were of a pagan origin, such as the Sheela-na-Gig, the hag with the yawning vulva who is probably a representation of the Crone aspect of the Goddess and Her sexuality: both these characteristics were rejected by Christianity. Also the Green Man, or foliate mask of the Nature God can be spotted in decoration. There are messages in the stonework, and it is probable that they are echoes of Palaeolithic whispers ….

Medicine Wheels and Native American Mounds

'Medicine wheels' are found in North America, from Canada to Colorado. These wheels can be up to 60 metres in diameter, made of stones, with spokes radiating from the centre to the perimeter. The Big Horn Medicine Wheel (Fig. 3.11) is perhaps the best known. It has 28 spokes, suggesting lunar associations, and 5 cairns around the circumference. However, one of the spokes was added in the twentieth century by 'restorers' who seem to have believed that the lunar 'month' was 28 days! In fact, as we have seen, there is no exact 28-day cycle of the moon, and those who originally set out the wheel may have done so with the express purpose of marking the 27-day sidereal cycle. This wheel is about 2,500 years old. Jay Ellis Ransom writes:

> *The archaeolinguistic artifact tells how the first people on earth … emerged as spirits out of the Underworld via a conduit topped by the large central rock cairn to become born as human beings. Where an offset cairn lies 12 feet outside the Wheel's rim, the greatly feared evil ghosts of the dead were uplifted into the Afterworld in the Milky Way … The rim of the structure*

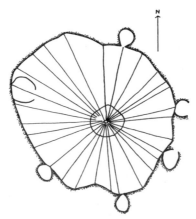

Figure 3.11 Big Horn Medicine Wheel

symbolized the cosmological horizon of the Milky Way ... All across Wyoming with radii up to 200 miles giant stone arrows direct the way to the Medicine Wheel to show the greatly feared evil ghosts of the dead the way to the Afterworld of Darkness. Thus the Medicine Wheel was also a mythological cemetery ... and a place totally lacking in religious sentiments.

Jay Ellis Ransom, *The Big Horn Medicine Wheel, The Birth & Death of Humanity,* Yellowstone Printing & Publishing, 1992, Cody, Wyoming 82414

From this account it would seem that the link between Native American medicine wheels and stone circles in the British Isles is tenuous. Some Native Americans have been accused of 'cashing in' on the New Age bandwagon in order to preserve sites which Ransom attests have no spiritual aspect, although it depends how we define 'spiritual'. It is unlikely that these Native American wheels have anything to do with the medicine wheel as a ritual, symbolic concept valued by shamanic practitioners today, but the arrows on the ground may link with the notion of 'spirit flight'. Present-day Native Americans seem to be estranged from the ancient civilisations that constructed these circles and earthworks, but there is no doubt that we can learn an immense amount from Native Americans with regard to attunement to and respect for the earth. Perhaps the jury is still out regarding these impressive structures. Could it be they will one day yield secrets as complex and profound as those of Stonehenge?

There are extensive earthworks in Marietta, Ohio, composed of mounds and ritual paths, laid out geometrically. The highest mound, over 10 metres in height, is called Conus. This site, now known to be about 2,000 years old, has been preserved, and was part of the Hopewell culture. Another earthwork called the Serpent Mound appears in Adams County, Ohio. This mound measures about 400 metres in length and is about 1.5 metres in height. The 'Serpent' has a spiralling tail and appears to have an egg in its mouth. The serpent is one of the oldest symbols relating to female sexuality, cycles and transformation. Snakes regularly slough off their skin; they disappear into the ground to re-emerge as if reborn. The spiral, formed often in nature and notably in the movement of water,

signifies passage into and out of the material world and suggests a cycle travelled in similar but progressing circles. It can represent an inward journey, similar to the more complex labyrinth, or maze.

Labyrinths

Labyrinths are found worldwide, depicted on rocks or in tombs, or cut into the turf. One of the best known is the terraced maze around Glastonbury Tor. There is also a labyrinth design on the floor of Chartres Cathedral. To the Hopi Indians the labyrinth was a sacred symbol of the Earth Mother, and two huge versions of the labyrinth are laid out on the Nazca plains. The spiral, a similar form of the maze, is widely used in the art and ritual of the Australian Aborigines. The closed spiral is said to represent the men of the Dreamtime who came up out of the earth. The most famous example is probably the labyrinth that features in the legend of Theseus and the Minotaur. Stan Gooch (see Further Reading) makes the point that a significant proportion of labyrinths display a left-handed first turning, which he links to the left-handedness of Neanderthal. The point of the true, older labyrinth, as opposed to the more confusing type made popular during recent centuries, is that there is only one way in and one way out. Walking or tracing the labyrinth can be a ritual or symbolic act, with mind-altering capabilities, and this could have formed part of initiation rites. The centre of the labyrinth may signify the womb of the Goddess or the depths of one's own being. These themes are echoed in the 'spiral dance' of witches. The labyrinth invites us to enter deep within ourselves in order to understand the hidden wisdom within the earth.

Terrestrial zodiacs

The most famous 'terrestrial zodiac' is that said to cluster around Glastonbury, where the twelve zodiacal symbols are laid out upon the land and delineated by a variety of factors such as names of

roads, hills and settlements. Since the 'discovery' of the Glastonbury zodiac, more than 60 others have been the subject of study. Ulrich Magin, in Issue 127 of *The Ley Hunter*, describes his experiment to construct an arbitrary zodiac around the village of Sternenfels in Germany. Sternenfels means 'Rock of the Stars' and was allegedly the site of a Megalithic pyramid. Magin found striking links similar to those around Glastonbury: for instance, on the horn of Capricorn is a hill called Horn and within the bow of Sagittarius lies 'Shooter's Lodge'. There is no doubt that it is all too easy to create the form one seeks from random shapes, and terrestrial zodiacs may seem highly questionable. However, one might also wonder what it is that led Magin to search in that particular place for a zodiac. Was it merely chance selection or some unrecognised intuition? Could Magin's position resemble that of the statistician Michel Gauquelin, who set out to disprove astrology and found instead that he had proved it? Perhaps the most important comment is made by Philip Heselton in *Elements of Earth Mysteries* (see Further Reading). He says:

> *We will fail to understand the significance of terrestrial zodiacs if we merely pick up on the generally insignificant evidence for their physical reality. It is a fundamental basis of the older religions and such crafts as astrology that there is ultimately no real distinction between that within us and that outside us ... terrestrial zodiacs can have a role regardless of whether they are considered objectively 'real' or not. Whether we discover them in the landscape or in ourselves, we are imbuing the places concerned with more significance than they would otherwise possess ... it is best to see them as a modern phenomenon and as part of a growing movement to find significance and variety in the landscape. If they can make us more aware of the Earth and our relationship with it then their study will have been worthwhile.*

In a similar way, the tarot and the Qabalistic Tree of Life with its many paths have been located within the landscape, notably by the writer Peter Morris. It seems such approaches are the literal ways our conscious mind employs to set up a connection between ourselves, the earth and the cosmos. They are valuable for their inspirational quality and their vivid, pictorial detail. If we take them literally we run the risk of fooling ourselves, and yet if we state 'It's just imagination'

we are devitalising the experience. For there is something numinous in the earth and our best course is to keep our eyes and ears open and retain our sense of wonderment and our ability to be amazed.

Hill figures

In southern England there are about 30 giant figures, carved into chalk hillsides, and evidence suggests that there may be many more that have become overgrown. White horses are the most frequently occurring figures, and of these the most famous is the Uffington White Horse, set within what appears to be a sacred landscape, with the ancient track of The Ridgeway running nearby, Dragon Hill in close proximity and the barrow called Wayland's Smithy about a mile away. This white horse is probably linked to Celtic horse-worship and to the goddesses Epona and Rhiannon. Obviously a valuable animal in the practical sense, the horse was regarded as a traveller between the worlds and a powerful totem beast – the drum of the shaman is called a 'horse' because the rhythm is a trigger to an altered state of consciousness. The Queen of Elphame is said to ride out from the barrow mounds on a white steed. In addition, the sexual symbolism of 'riding' is obvious and hence is a connection with fertility. Celtic kings were confirmed in office by the sacrifice of a horse, from whose meat a broth was made in which the king bathed and drank – totem animals could usually be killed and eaten only for strict ritual purposes. Blacksmiths, because of their transformative work with metals, were considered magical, and themes of melting down and reforming appear in shamanic trance experience. (Wayland was the Norse god of smithcraft, and local legend stated that a horse left by Wayland's Smithy on the night of the full moon would be magically shod with silver.) Here we have a train of associations suggesting the sacred and 'spiritual' character of the Uffington White Horse landscape, something of which I have certainly had personal experiences.

The White Horse can be seen properly only from above, suggesting that it was designed to be seen by space travellers, and it also has a connection with shamanic flight. Other figures include giants, such

as the Long Man of Wilmington in East Sussex and the ithyphallic Cerne Abbas giant in Dorset, treasured for his 'fertile' powers. Some figures are of relatively recent origin, although their precise antiquity cannot be ascertained, as they survive only by being maintained regularly. As far as I am aware, there is nothing quite like those figures in the rest of the world, possibly because chalk hillside is the best medium on which to fashion them. However, the Nazca geoglyphs are similar, with lines that seem to have been constructed in order to be seen primarily from above. Michael Howard in *Earth Mysteries* (see Further Reading) has this to say:

> *It is certain that the hill figures of southern England were an attempt by the ancient people who carved them to bring the old gods down to earth … These figures became the focus of powerful rituals designed to unlock the geomantic forces which permeated the landscape and were symbolised by the sacred images carved in the hillsides.*

By the interaction of human and land the old gods were conjured into manifestation – and they are still with us, waking from their sleep … .

Sacred Landscapes

Many landscapes appear to be of themselves sacred. Notably, around Glastonbury, also known as the Isle of Avalon, the contours of the birth-giving goddess can be discerned. Such landscapes may be detected all over the place where the soul of the human and the soul of the land intertwine. Two further examples are the ancient civilisation of Crete and the land around Eleusis, in Greece, home of the mystery cult. Mountains with double peaks, suggesting breasts – or perhaps the cradle of the womb – were a favoured symbol, and sanctuaries and temples were erected to harmonise with the natural structure.

Natural formations such as wells and caves often have a powerful presence. Wells, where the life-giving spring of the goddess comes to the surface, are often considered healing sites. Their atmosphere is

charged with aeons of pilgrimage and worship, dreamings, and the sweet out-breath of the earth. Chalice Well in Glastonbury is one such example: in the Gardens of the Chalice Well it is impossible for most people to maintain the mind-set of the day to day; instead one drifts into an expanded, timeless consciousness. Wells were – and are – often 'dressed' at times of festival, with flowers and offerings, and those seeking healing could come to the well, dip a piece of cloth in the waters and tie this to a nearby tree, as an offering or an act of symbolic cleansing. Wells have long been considered sacred to the Goddess, especially Celtic Bride, the waters equating with health, the flow of milk or with amniotic fluid.

Caves, mountain tops and waterfalls are all places where natural ionisation occurs, and this can affect the brain function of people in the area. Caves have an obvious association with the womb of the Great Mother and have been used to induce altered states of consciousness, and in shamanic initiation rites – here we may find 'rebirth' in a spiritual sense. Artificial structures such as barrows and cromlechs can provide a similar function. Groves of trees also have an aura that is awesome and moving – their scent and their presence seem to bypass the conscious mind and to speak to something within that is primeval. Certain combinations of trees may have special meanings, for instance the 'fairy triad' of oak and ash and thorn, or groupings of trees that include the Celtic tree alphabet as described by Robert Graves. In all these places, and in many different ways, the earth speaks to us.

LANDSCAPES OF THE ABORIGINES

The most vivid tradition of living landscape is demonstrated by the Australian Aborigines. All over the Outback, natural features mark the emergence and the activities of Dreamtime ancestors. For instance, two boys, of the Dreamtime ancestors, formed Uluru (Ayers Rock) (Fig. 3.12) in the deserts of Central Australia. However, although these dramas occurred in a mythic past, the Aborigines still do not apparently share the concept of linear time so intrinsic to the modern world. The Dreamtime is not some long-gone history that

Figure 3.12 Ayers Rock

has dimmed to myth, but is, in a sense, a continuous present existing in a shifted dimension. As the Aborigine travels over the terrain, the legendary journeys of the Ancestors are recreated by song and ritual. The arduous initiatory experiences of young Aboriginal men acquired power only at sacred, totem sites where the *altirangamatjina*, or the Dreamtime beings, dwelt. A power, or an essence existed at these sites and could be accessed by song and ritual – this essence was called *kurunba*, and the sacred sites were called 'increase centres'. Paul Devereux, in *Earth Memory* (see Further Reading) writes:

> *Around Midwinter an increase ceremony takes … place at Ngama, an outcrop of rocks near Mount Eclipse in central Australia. A low, isolated rocky hill a few hundred yards west of Ngama is where Malatji, leader of the mystical Dog-people and his clan, made camp during the Dreamtime. A boulder on this hillock is 'a concentrated mass of the life-essence or kurunba of wild dogs'. In the increase ceremony, an aboriginal Elder, taking a piece of rock and chanting the appropriate songs, breaks off pieces of the boulder, causing kurunba to permeate the environment, fertilising the female dogs of the region … the kurunba spread through the air 'like a mist'.*

We shouldn't deduce from this that the Aborigines are confused about myth and reality for they are clear about the actual processes of nature in the environment. However, the 'real' landscape is permeated by the landscape of legend, and animated by it. This 'dreaming' capacity is what we have largely lost and what we seek to recreate and reclaim in landscapes of the Goddess and the Hero.

Ðealing the split

It has been suggested by Julian Jaynes (in *The Origin of Consciousness in the Breakdown of the Bicameral Mind*, 1976) that the ancients possessed a type of split consciousness, where the temporal lobes of the brain were connected across the anterior commissure between the two hemispheres. Because of this, part of their brains would have spoken to them in the form of 'voices' similar to the experience of a schizoprenic. This amounted to the voices of the gods, heard by heroes of Greek legend and the like. It is well known today that the right and left sides of the brain perform different functions. The right brain corresponds to the left side of the body and is concerned with intuitions and patterns, whereas the left brain is more logical and controls the right side. Hemisphere functions are reversed in left-handed people, although left-handedness has been connected to artistic and instinctual abilities – and Neanderthal is believed to have been left-handed. The ability to hear the 'voices' may have been lost abruptly, resulting in the forsaking of ancient sites, where the skulls of the ancestors had formerly 'spoken'. However, the ability to 'hear' and to prophecy would have been retained (and arguably still is) by persons of special talent.

Sites that are/were sacred or in some way special have been chosen as burial sites, probably for a variety of reasons, ranging from simple respect (or even fear) through the wish to choose the most favourable site for rebirth, as in the womb of the Mother, to an attitude of ancestor-worship, thus wishing to house the venerable skulls where their wisdom could be best accessed. This 'access'

seems to me to be gained most easily in what we refer to as sacred sites, both natural and constructed. In certain places the primeval forces of the cosmos, of birth, sex and death seem also to be concentrated. This may be linked to ionisation, radiation or similar, or may be much more subtle. However, a change in consciousness can be triggered and the basic force here seems to be to do with transformation of some kind.

I experienced this in 1996 when on a tour of 'Shamanic Gateways' – barrows and standing stones – in the Cotswolds in the west of England, led by Danny Sullivan, editor of *The Ley Hunter*. While examining the remains of Uley Long Barrow I was dowsing, and as the rods crossed I experienced a joyful and decidedly sexual feeling. Just as this happened a woman near me asked 'Oooh, did you feel that?' 'What?' I said. 'I don't know,' she replied, 'all I can say is that it felt the same as really good sex!' I have experienced similar sensations at other ancient sites. Our most vivid experiences, when we feel most invaded and elevated by forces that seem to come from outside us, are when giving birth (or participating in the experience) or when having 'really good' sex. The ultimate experience of this nature is probably encountered at death. I have found that shamanic experience may be linked to states of sexual arousal and when we dream we are sexually aroused. Barrow mounds, cromlechs, caves, etc., may be sites for shamanic initiation, which is a type of 'death' as orgasm has been called 'the little death'.

So our special places of antiquity seem to have a unifying quality, bridging the gap, so that our instinctual selves may speak to us, bringing together earth, human and cosmos and linking levels of experience in a transcendent union. Here we may find life at its most vivid and understand why the sexual act was and is considered sacred by pagans, for it is connected to more than fertility – in certain circumstances it is part of a passage to the divine.

PRACTICE

In this chapter we have found awesome associations in stone circles and simple geometry with cosmic cycles. We have looked at landscapes as living patterns and wondered about their ability to change our consciousness. Finally we have even considered that a simple mound of earth may be connected, and have powers to activate, primordial and transformative experiences in ourselves, to do with our sexuality, dissolution and rebirth. Is this too much? Does the earth-song open caverns within you? Or are these just interesting or pretty places to visit? Whatever the case, seek out an ancient, or remarkable site near you, visit it and take note. If there are no traditional or historic places nearby, go to one that is beautiful, outstanding or 'feels special' – this could be near to a special tree, or trees, a hill top with a view, a riverside, waterfall, large boulder or just the corner of a field. How do you feel? Is there something different about this place? Can you define or describe it? Spend some time seeking out 'special' places nearby, either by visiting and exploring or doing some detective work with local history. Whatever happens, your sense of your locality is sure to be enhanced.

Great God Cernunnos, return to earth again! ...
Open the door, the door that hath no key,
The door of dreams whereby men come to thee ...

From a Wiccan ritual

The olD faith

The old religion of paganism is based upon worship of the earth and the cycle of the seasons. When we speak of this we are, in fact, covering a broad area, and many thousands of years, for Christianity and other forms of patriarchal monotheism are relative

newcomers on the globe. These ancient faiths comprised 'animism', 'pantheism' and 'polytheism'. Animism put simply means that 'all is alive', and that includes wind and rain, the rushing stream and the moody rock. Only slightly removed from this is the idea that 'all is divine' or 'god is everywhere' which is pantheism. Polytheism means 'many gods': in a diverse, animate creation goddesses and gods are everywhere, taking many forms and personifying elemental forces and a sense of the numinous. These beliefs have been dubbed primitive, and yet they convey an all-pervading sense of the sacred and a land that pulsed with divine presence. Over the last 2,000 years we have lost a great deal in our separation of divinity from matter, for the natural world has lost its soul – officially. 'God's in His heaven' but all is *not* right with a world that is regarded as base, there to be used, abused and subdued. As for the Goddess, whose body was the earth and whose blessing fell in each raindrop – where is she? Our sense of the spirit in soil, tree, flower and cloud have departed with her, along with our sense of wonderment and of belonging. Many people feel this lack, although comparatively few might put it that way.

Currently, paganism is undergoing a considerable revival, in many forms. This is a religion with no dogma and only one exhortation – 'Harm none'. Pagans seek to rediscover old traditions and wisdom and refurbish them in a modern context. The point here is not to be sentimental and idealistic about barbaric cultures, which practised human sacrifice and lived lives that were extremely uncomfortable and fear-ridden, but rather to retrieve what is valuable and has been lost. Loving and honouring the earth as mother Goddess, pagans celebrate and enjoy the seasonal cycle and also find both the pleasurable and the divine in the human body itself, as a gift of the Goddess. Most pagans take an especial pleasure in contact with nature. Of course, 'fresh air' and 'getting out into the country' are something of a cultural obsession to our urban society but to pagans there is more to it than that, for they seek a sense of mystical attunement and belonging in places of natural beauty – contact with nature is an act of worship. The seasonal cycle is usually explicitly honoured in the eight festivals: Yule (22 December); Imbolc (2 February); Spring Equinox (21 March); Beltane (30 April); Midsummer (22 June); Lughnasadh (31 July); Autumn Equinox

(21 September); Samhain or Hallowe'en (31 October). These festivals are moved forward or backward six months in the Southern Hemisphere. Generally considered to be Celtic in origin, each festival celebrates a different point in the 'love story' of the Goddess and God.

The Goddess can be considered as the cycle itself, while the God is He who travels. The Goddess, as the earth, changes Her face but not Her essence, while the God, as the sun, waxes and wanes in strength throughout the year. The God is considered to be the Sun-Lover of the Goddess who gives birth to Him anew each year, and this is paralleled in many specific stories such as that of Venus and Adonis, Cybele and Attis, Isis and Osiris/Horus. Born (usually) at Yule, the God grows through the festivals of Imbolc and Spring Equinox to take His place as the lover of the Goddess at Beltane and Midsummer. At Lughnasadh He is cut down as the Corn Spirit and becomes King of the Underworld at Samhain, only to be born again at Yule, Son of His own fathering. Of course, no literal incest is implied here, simply cyclicity. Naturally, there are many variations and permutations upon the 'story' and different pagans did and do celebrate and worship in different ways – some think principally in terms of the changing face of the Earth Mother alone. However we look at it, it is a way of bringing to life our sense of the sacred in the natural world. It is also worth noting that in many mythologies the sun was feminine and the moon – taken these days as the celestial manifestation of the Goddess – was masculine. (Indeed, it is the case that almost all Aboriginal tribes regard the sun as feminine.) However, we do not have to be exact. For our purposes here the point is that religion and the most vivid forms of spirituality can be seen as arising from within the earth and her seasons. Paganism is arguably an active participation in 'earth mysteries'. (Modern paganism is fully discussed in *Paganism – a beginner's guide* in this series.)

Customs and rituals

Arising from the seasonal cycle many local customs still prevail, although their original meaning may have been lost. One of the best known of these is dancing around the maypole on May Day. The

sexual significance of the phallic maypole in the receptive earth is obvious. The pattern of the dancing feet of the revellers may be detected by dowsers. May Day is also celebrated in Padstow, Cornwall by the antics of the 'Obby 'Oss. Another example of a local festival still celebrated is the Abbots Bromley Horn Dance which occurs about two weeks before the Autumn Equinox. Here in the Cotswolds the younger local children go out in spring to 'wake up the trees', rapping their trunks and crying 'Bud well, bear well, wake up in the morning' – a custom revived by a headteacher who obviously wanted to reaffirm contact with nature, in some fashion, for the children. We have already seen how sites of antiquity mark significant points in the passage of the seasons. The astronomer Norman Lockyer has suggested that Stonehenge was a temple for sun worship, aligned to sunrise and sunset on the quarter days. These 'quarter days' – Beltane, Lughnasadh, Samhain and Imbolc – are often regarded as the main festivals, all celebrated by fire and historically preceding the Solstice and Equinox feast days, that became more important with the progress of agriculture. The St Michaels ley line, that we encountered in Chapter 1, is aligned to the May Day sunrise.

For the Aboriginal peoples, story, song, ritual and the land are inseparable. The *karadji*, or person of high degree, has direct contact with the spirits of the Dreaming, and he is therefore the only one who can create new chants and dances – he is in intimate relationship with the spirit of the land. We have already seen, in Chapter 3, how time of year affects Aboriginal ceremonies when we looked at the 'increase ceremony' near Mount Eclipse, at Midwinter.

In America there are many examples, one being at Cahokia in Illinois, where there is a complex of mounds, the largest being Monk's Mound. These show alignments to sunrise at the Equinoxes and Solstices and orientation to the cardinal directions. These four directions, in another context, from the basis of the ritual device of the medicine wheel, or power wheel, that Westerners are now borrowing from Native American tradition. Customs and rituals linking human activity with the land and the cycles of the sky appear all over the globe and seem basic to human response.

Nature spirits

The pagan Goddess and God are manifest in the earth and her cycles, and in one sense they can be seen as a vitalisation of the numinous powers in Creation, anthropomorphised. However, in folklore and in the beliefs of many modern pagans – and some country people – spirits of a more modest but explicit kind exist. In other words, fairies. It may be hard to accept the existence of fairies because they have been the subject of ridicule and hoaxes. Nonetheless, there are those who insist fairies are real, and there are also those who claim to have seen fairies. We are talking here of a nature spirit, a breath of the living land. Traditionally, there are four types of 'elemental': gnomes (spirits of earth); sylphs (spirits of air); salamanders (spirits of fire); undines (spirits of water). These are invoked in magical rites, but their presence can also be felt in natural locations, as you will find if you still your mind near peaceful waters, in your garden or on a windy hilltop. In addition, there are dryads who guard trees, naiads who inhabit waterfalls, nereids by the sea, and oreads in mountainous or desert regions.

Nature spirits of a type, but rather more graphic, are depicted in Aboriginal rock art in Kakadu National Park in Northern Territory. Some of these paintings are carbon dated to more than 20,000 years old. One of the paintings is of the Rainbow Serpent. Thousands of years ago this serpent was ceremonially tapped with sticks in order to release spirits into nearby billabongs, to grow into water snakes which was a favourite Aboriginal food. At Nourlangie Rock, Namarrgon, the Lightning Man dwells, immortalised in rock art. In the dark of a storm, Aborigines would shelter against the rock and watch him make lightning by striking his two stone axes together. These can be seen as human instinctual identification of natural forces and objectification of them in art.

Less majestic British tales abound, of 'little men' who appear near barrow mounds and who must be treated with respect, in order to avoid harm. Stories of fairy revels in their subterranean dwellings are frequent. Travellers who visit the fairies must be careful not to eat or drink anything, or the traveller will be lost forever to the

mortal world. These barrow-dwellers are called by the Irish the people of the Sidhe (pronounced *shee*) – magical and eerie – or they are held by some to be the pre-Celtic people who remained close to the land, living within it and somehow slipping into another dimension, hidden from the eyes of mortals. Fairies were known to dance around the King Stone – the outlying stone – at the Rollright Circle in Oxfordshire. They have also been seen at Pentre Ifan cromlech, in Dyfed, Wales, which is also called 'the Cauldron of Cerridwen'. Cerridwen is an underworld goddess, and Pentre Ifan was an initiation site. The Music Barrow on Binchcombe Down, Dorset, has the reputation of being inhabited by fairy musicians, playing beneath the earth, and if you put your ear to the barrow at midday you can hear them. These are just a few of many such tales.

Barrows were often thought to be entrances to the Otherworld; this may link with their properties as 'shamanic gateways'. The fairies are considered by some people to be a personification of the energies within the land and the power of these energies to change human consciousness. Other people prefer a more literal explanation. One thing is certain, however – the magical quality with which such tales endow the land is a reality and there to be experienced.

healing and petrifying

Ancient sites often have a reputation for the manifestation of healing qualities, perhaps necessitating crawling through a hole in a stone. Men-an-Tol in Cornwall is a famous example, where sick children were passed through the large hole in the centre of the circular stone. The Holey Stone on Minchinhampton Common in Gloucestershire was reputed to heal children with measles and whooping cough; I can only deduce from the size of the hole that children were considerably smaller and thinner in days of yore! Other stones necessitated those to be healed crawling around them, a certain number of times at a specified time of day and year. Fertility, too, was bestowed by the stones; the stones at the circle at Avebury in Wiltshire are alternately diamond shaped and phallus shaped, representing the female and the male genitalia. Tales of

special gifts attached to stones are many and varied, including the ability to bestow good fortune and alter mental states. Healing powers are also often especially attributed to wells.

In addition, many stone circles are linked with stories of people who were turned to stone, often as a punishment for dancing on the Sabbath. The majestic stone at Catchall, near Penzance in Cornwall, is said to be a fiddler turned to stone for playing on a Sunday, and the Nine Maidens on Belstone Common near Okehampton, Devon, were turned to stone for Sunday frolicking, and legend tells that they dance again, daily at noon. As far afield as Senegambia in West Africa, it is believed that the Kaur stone circle is a wedding party, turned to stone for celebrating into the early hours of the Sabbath. Stories also tell of stones that move periodically, of their own accord, often on special dates such as Midsummer's Day. All such tales would seem to suggest that some sort of 'life' is sensed within the stones, rather ironically twisted to a punitive theme by Christian thought, which often tended to demonise the ancient relics of pagan forbears, while taking over their sites. At Stanton Drew, in Avon, a shadowy fiddler appeared to a wedding party and played on into Sunday morning. The fiddler was, of course, the Devil (another favourite character in this type of lore) and all the guests were turned into the stones. Stanton Drew church stands on the site.

Dragons and giants

Dragons feature in many stories about places of antiquity and it is the power of the dragon that sleeps within the earth. The breath of the dragon rises as mist that clothes the mounds and stones. Many stories tell of the slaying of dragons, notably by St George (who, although he is England's patron saint, probably never visited England in reality). St George's notable exploit is said in local legend to have taken place on Dragon Hill, close by the Uffington White Horse; a patch of grassless soil marks the spot where the dragon's blood fell. George's name is interesting, for 'ge' meant earth (as in 'geology, geography'). The warlike and heroic theme of slaying may be a metaphor for regulation of the mighty earth currents as

75

symbolised by the dragon. Of course, the dragon could also be the old Great Mother Goddess 'vanquished' by the heroes of patriarchy: the story of Tiamat, Babylonian dragon-goddess of the primordial deeps, is one such. She was killed by her great-great-great grandson, Marduk, and her body was used to make the firmament. The forces in the Chinese system of geomancy, Feng Shui, are personified as the Azure Dragon and the White Tiger. Of course, it is also possible that dragons were/are real creatures, and the controversial Scottish Loch Ness Monster may be one!

Giants, with their superhuman strength, are often said to have been responsible for the placing of large stones or natural features. Often the stones were believed to have been carried in the apron of a giant, or giantess, hence such names as Apron String, near Mullion in Cornwall, and the Great Apronful and Little Apronful, near Ilkley, West Yorkshire. 'Giants' also appear in the great hill figures such as the Cerne Abbas giant and the Long Man of Wilmington in East Sussex. Giant beings feature in Aboriginal lore, loving, lusting, fighting and heaving mountains from the earth during their battles. These giants may be a dim memory of people who were stronger and more knowledgeable about the powers of nature, and so seemed superhuman. Again, the concept of a giant, with huge strength, could be a way of personifying earth forces – either those felt in an abstract sense, or related to phenomena such as earthquakes.

Ghosts and ghouls

The ghouls of horror film are gruesome, undead beings who prey on human flesh. However, the ghouls we are considering here prey rather on human emotions. The dowser, Tom Lethbridge, postulated an energy field around each human being that arises from their emotional state and that most, if not all, hauntings arise from an interaction between this personal field and the force field of the earth itself. This earth force is concentrated – as we have seen in other contexts – around waterfalls, springs, certain trees, woodland, moor, mountain, shore and stream. Lethbridge classified the earth

force according to the dryads, nereids, etc. that we met earlier in this chapter, and these are all seemingly associated with underground water. Water in the atmosphere can also be a trigger, and we are all familiar with the Gothic scenario of the misty day, when the phantom appears. If a 'leakage' takes place between the personal field of a human and a place where the earth force is strong, then the place will be 'impressed' with the image or feeling, rather like a film.

Ghosts may be explained as stored pictures – what the person saw – while ghouls are records of what someone felt. A notable example is of the 'Ladram Bay ghoul'. Ladram Bay is the scene of repeated suicides where people experienced a feeling of extreme heaviness and sensed that something was encouraging them to jump off the cliff. Such ghouls and ghosts are not nature spirits, but a subtle product of the interaction between human and environment. However, Lethbridge did choose nature-spirit names for his earth-energy fields. If we believe in nature spirits we might also consider the possibility that some are less than well disposed towards humans! Ghosts are often seen at ancient sites, such as Avebury. In Australia, Kata Tjuta (or Mount Olga), 50 km east of Ayers Rock, is a notable haunt of dead spirits, its traditional name translating as 'many heads'. Native American medicine wheels may also be haunts of the dead. Many places have an eerie reputation, and it is worth researching the tales relevant to your own locality to see what emerges, and whether your own experiences can back them up.

The ϝINϭhORN COϭϭUNITY

The Findhorn Community was founded in Scotland in 1962, by a group of individuals who wished to live close to nature and in harmony with her ways. From the relationships with spirits of nature that were developed, some notable results were achieved, not only in growing giant vegetable specimens in a hostile environment, but also by exciting co-operation from animals. For instance, moles were persuaded to leave the garden by a communication – perhaps 'shamanic journey' would be a better term – to the 'Mole King' who

agreed that his people would leave for the scrubland adjacent. Three 'kingdoms' in the hierarchy of nature spirits were identified at Findhorn: the nature spirits or elementals; the devas who are a sort of 'landscape angel'; and nature itself. The devas are the essences behind each place and they lay the pattern upon which the energy forms or elementals build. This is reminiscent of Sheldrake's 'morphogenetic fields'. Nature itself just *is*, everywhere. The elementals perform the routine maintenance work, and together they are represented by the great god Pan. The Findhorn Community is evidence of what can be achieved if humans will only approach nature in an attitude of respect. Of course, all this sounds like mumbo-jumbo in the face of combine harvesters and factory farming. However, it is worth nothing that our progress is not so brilliant. If you discount problems such as BSE and controversies over genetic manipulation of crops and the like our life expectancy has not increased impressively compared to the Third World or our own ancestors. The reason why, statistically, it *looks* good is due mainly to the decrease in perinatal mortality. Neither are our longer lives ones of happiness. Something is amiss. It seems obvious to look to our roots and to the land for answers.

PRACTICE

Have you had a 'strange' experience linked significantly to the place you were when it happened? Was there a 'ley-line' running close by? Or some ancient monument in close proximity? Have other people had similar experiences in this place?

Research the folklore of your district or talk to people whose families have lived there, possibly for generations. Whatever part of the world you inhabit, there is sure to be a wealth of stories attached to the landscape and any ancient structure thereon. Those of you who live in Australia or America may be doubly fortunate in that you have the lore of Aborigines or Native Americans – arguably more immediate than British or European folk tales – on which to draw.

5 ΤΗΕ SPIRIT OF ΤΗΕ ΕΑRΤΗ

… And round and round the circle spun
Until the gates swung wide ajar
That bar the boundaries of earth
From faery realms that shine afar …

… For I have been beyond the town
Where meadowsweet and roses grow,
And there such music did I hear
As worldly-righteous never know

Doreen Valiente, *The Witch's Ballad*

The earth spirit is everywhere. By glistening stream or pewter ocean, it is our watchful companion; it breathes softly in forest

glade and meadow and its deep laughter echoes over the hill and mountain. It seems often as if there are many earth spirits, wild and wise, mirthful, protective, benevolent, shy – and sometimes cold, even ruthless towards the paltriness of our humanity. But mostly the earth spirit is about love, beauty and a profound acceptance. There may be a multitude, or there may be just one – Goddess of Many Faces, and a single essence. One of Her names is Gaia.

Gaia

The Greek name for the Earth Mother was Gaia, titaness and Creatrix. This name has become well known since the 1970s, when the biologist James Lovelock put forward the idea that the life of the earth functions as a single organism, defining and maintaining the conditions for its continuing survival. According to this theory, earth is not merely a conglomeration of rock, sludge and water that brought forth life in due course through the laws of chance but a self-regulating and in some way sentient being that may be evolving humans as a 'nervous system'. Human technology may soon be advanced enough to enable us to save Gaia, in circumstances such as collision with a large meteor. Of course, humans can also wreak havoc and destruction, and to date our track record is not good. This book began by mentioning the image of our beautiful planet as she is seen from space. That is Gaia. It is almost as if we have had to leave her to appreciate her; as if we had to achieve a detached perspective in order to allow the life within us to recognise the life that is hers.

The vitality of Gaia is all around us, interpenetrating and nourishing our own. We feel her in our bones, and we are never alone, because when there are no other humans with us then are we most conscious of her vast and peaceful presence. Just as humans have an aura, or energy field, surrounding their bodies, so too Gaia has an aura. This is more than the atmosphere that surrounds her, stretching for miles into space, it is something more subtle, but yet we breathe it and

live and move within it. Humans also have subtle power centres, or chakras, that are involved in the circulation of energy. It seems that Gaia too has 'power centres' called earth chakras, and these are points on the earth where the force field is felt most intensely, usually as a healing influence. However, although Gaia is, to us, a Goddess, we must be wary of being too literal in our anthropomorphising of Her. Her chakras are not necessarily a parallel to our own: in Britain alone there is an enormous number of 'heart chakras', targeted as prime sites to heal and save the world. All we need to know is that the earth is special, and to honour our instincts about places that feel highly charged, for this sense is partly personal, partly general – but this sense and these places are our connections with the divinity that is Gaia.

Not only is the earth conscious, but it seems we may inhabit a conscious universe. The symmetry of the sun/earth/moon system that we encountered in Chapter 3 suggest that 'God is a geometer' and this is encoded in the structure of Stonehenge. In many places and in many ways our world speaks to us the ancient message of the sages 'All is alive' and encourages us to expand ourselves to encompass that fact.

eLf

Our concept of Gaia as the Earth Mother has a basis in our subliminal experience, for just as a baby in the womb is surrounded by the rhythmic beat of its mother's heart, so are we enveloped in the heartbeat of the earth. The earth resonates perpetually to an extremely low frequency (ELF), produced from a variety of sources but principally from outer space. Interestingly, the frequencies emitted by the brain are within the ELF range. The Delta rhythm (0.5–4 Hz) is equated with higher levels of consciousness. The Theta rhythm (4–7 Hz) along with the Delta rhythm is connected with dreaming. (Other rhythms are Alpha, 8–13 Hz, and Beta, 13–30 Hz; these are connected to different levels of activity). So, vibrationally, we are part of the earth and we resonate with her.

Our states of expanded awareness are intimately connected with earth's functions, and if we seek 'spiritual experience' from enlightenment to shamanic flight, we are arguably entering into closer communion with the earth. Could this be why the Apollo astronauts claimed to have developed extra-sensory perceptions or had 'strange' experiences? Does the temporary disorientation of leaving the earth sharpen one's responses on return? (And if so, would it not be a valid area of research to try to get some idea of what will happen to humans who venture truly outside the heartbeat and the orbit of Gaia, further into space?)

David Elkington, in his article 'Blessed Mary, Mother of Science' (*Quest* magazine, Apr/May 1996) points out that:

As we have evolved into her natural embrace we have developed a considerable relationship with what is in effect our 'Mother'. Is this the reason why she should appear to those that would see her, as female? Is it not the mother that scolds the naughty child?

The reason for her appearances to date could be that we have consciously chosen to ignore her … Sometimes the best way to communicate is literally and the realm of the faithful is the only channel that remains open. It is the oldest.

Here David is referring to supernatural sightings, usually of the Virgin Mary, such as that at Lourdes in 1858 or Medjugorje, Yugoslavia, in the early 1980s. Although Mary is not officially a goddess, she is the closest image available in many countries for the Divine Feminine. He continues:

Given that the earth resonates outwardly through space, inwardly her resonance gains form at … specific sites … It would not be fanciful to point out that many churches and Dolmenic chambers are in actuality resonators. Holy places, where ancient minds, educated in the ways of the earth … communed with their God; a fusion of Earth and Cosmic forces.

We are back again with our sacred sites, but with a clearer message that someone may be literally trying to communicate with us.

Green spirituality

In Chapter 4 we touched on the meaning of paganism. One of the important points about paganism is that it is about what you do and feel, rather than about laws and dogma. The material world has been demonised and degraded by systems that look upwards and beyond for transcendence and equate the spiritual solely with the non-material. Pagans seek to venerate the earth, not merely by ritual, celebration or even mystical experience, but also in a practical sense, by looking after her. This is common sense, of course, because earth is our home, but it can be accomplished only by love and identification. Unless we revere the earth and approach her with humility, as goddess at least in some fashion, we will find it well-nigh impossible to leave behind our arrogant belief that exploitation is justified because the intellect of humankind will triumph over Nature. It won't. It is probably no exaggeration to say that unless we appreciate the full extent of our dependence upon Gaia and her power, then we as a race are doomed.

Because of this it would seem that we are called upon to live responsibly, attempting to give back to the planet that maintains us and refraining from abusing her. Of course, we cannot accomplish miracles, nor need we become neurotic concerning the impact of our actions – but many things are common sense, such as re-using, recycling, preservation of trees and the environment generally, avoidance of chemicals, pesticides, etc., limiting car use. It would seem that respect is the keynote, and again an awareness that the earth is goddess. Only at your peril do you abuse and pillage a deity, and earth is tolerant, like most mothers. However, a thump from an irate toddler is quite different from a threat by an adolescent. In our reckless progress through genetic engineering, cloning and all manner of modern scientific manipulation, we are behaving like clever and irresponsible adolescents. This is not to oppose progress – the important attitude is surely respect, and humility. We do not – cannot – know what we are doing, until future generations have passed their verdict. Already, the flood of female hormones from

synthetic preparations into the ecosystem is affecting male fertility – something that was not anticipated. Probably this is the tip of the iceberg. The Findhorn Community displayed what humans can do when acting in harmony with nature. Pagans, with 'green spirituality' are showing how to live and act in honour of the earth – this is a vital part of our relationship with her and our participation in her 'mystery'.

Developing a personal response

We saw in Chapter 3 how entire landscapes acquire a sacred characteristic by the discernment of the contours of the Goddess in their natural features. The countryside around Glastonbury is one notable example. However, we may also find ourselves in the presence of the divine when we are in other localities. Pregnant belly, breast, thigh, phallic shapes and faces can be found in many shapes in nature, including hills, valleys, rocks and tree-trunks. We have a tendency to look for human figures – it is natural for the eye to discern them. However, there is more here than an impulse to find the human form everywhere. This is the way of the earth to communicate with us and our way of tuning in to such messages. By looking at the landscape in this way we can develop a sense of being nurtured and held, and a profound communion. Indeed, we can form a proper relationship with the land.

Human-made structures are often reminiscent of the shapes mentioned above, and Silbury Hill has been often likened to the pregnant belly of the Earth Mother, although Shuttle and Redgrove in *The Wise Wound* liken Silbury Hill to the cervix, or neck of the womb. I am sure the ancients were well-enough acquainted with the characteristics of their own bodies to create this.

However, we like to think of it, the landscape will paint pictures for us, if we let it. Flowing female contours obviously suggest themselves, but that is not necessarily how the land will appear to you – let

yourself see the landscape as it is revealed to you, however this may be. We do not have to follow the ideas of anyone else in this respect. It is good to sit in a place of your own choosing, quietly and peacefully, and just *look* – not 'for' anything, but just 'at'. The emotions and visions that arise in this way may be surprising and vivid.

A special place

Many people who love the land find they have a special 'place' where the earth seems to speak to them with particular intimacy. Children are often good at finding such places, and calling them 'dens'. Animals, too, are no doubt drawn to certain sites that in some way resonate to their life-force or purpose: animals have a sense of place and the stored essence of the earth, which may be human induced – birds avoid flying over the sites of concentration camps, like Belsen, for instance.

Through life we may find a succession of special locations that serve this purpose. My own 'place' is a small valley in the Cotswolds where a breath of peace and a thrill of wonderment invariably come upon me whenever I visit. There is such vibrant life in each tree, plant and stone, and from the corner of my eye I may catch the graceful movement of the entities of the land. A stream gurgles through, over rocks and pebbles – always changing, always the same. When the rain falls the place rings and tinkles as if every faery bell in creation were pealing out. In autumn, the breath of the dying year exhales a mist that shrouds the low places, that are gateways to the Mysteries. And when the full moon traces a silver filigree through the trees, my heart is filled with poetry and worship. When I am sad or stressed I can travel, inwardly, to this place and feel comforted. I feel privileged to know of it.

If you find a special place it is a gift, and your gift, in return, is your joy and enjoyment which mingle with its character and may be passed on to others who follow in your footsteps. The fact that it is possible to dowse where others have trodden indicates that where we have been, how we have felt is stored in the memory of the

landscape. Each person will have a different response to a locality. It is likely that our forbears created their structures from a spontaneous and instinctive response that to them would have been so vivid as to have seemed almost a command. Rock art, such as that of the Aborigines probably originated in a similar way. It is hardly fitting – nor can we trust our modern perceptions – to respond in like manner. However, we may find that special sites inspire us to poetry, painting, sculpture or other forms of art. It seems to me that much of art is the natural world speaking through us and seeking other forms and expressions of itself through the medium of the human.

In *Secret Places of the Goddess* (see Further Reading) Philip Heselton lists the following things you may want from a 'special place': somewhere where your spirits are uplifted and you can feel positive; somewhere to meditate; somewhere conducive to attaining 'cosmic consciousness'; somewhere to sleep to bring prophetic dreams; somewhere to achieve an initiatory experience; somewhere for intimate conversation, counselling or healing; somewhere to perform seasonal or magical rituals; somewhere to make love; somewhere to meet the Old Gods and elemental beings in an atmosphere of trust. There may be other things you want from your special site. As long as they are about love and 'harm none', you will find your site.

What you find in your special place may be meaningful to you; I have found amazing stones in the shape of goddess-forms, in my valley. However, we must be careful what we take from nature, and while there can be nothing wrong in picking up a few stones in a little visited location, it is best to take nothing at all from ancient sites that receive a lot of visitors. For instance, if everyone took a pebble or two from Silbury Hill in the Avebury complex, the place would be denuded! Common sense and – again – respect, are the correct approaches.

TENDING A SITE

One practical 'act of worship' is to look after a site, picking up litter and generally getting in tune, so that one has a sense of what the

place 'needs' as an expression of its essence. It may be appropriate to clear some areas so that certain plants may flourish, a stream may flow freely or a standing stone may become more obvious, but such decisions can and should be made only after one has taken plenty of time to get to know the wishes of the nature spirits that are guardians of the place, for their permission should be asked. If you are not conscious of, or you do not believe in such 'spirits' then I am sure you will, as a lover of the earth, still appreciate the need to get in touch with what the site needs, rather than what we, as humans, would like to impose upon it. If you have the time you may like to embark upon a project to clear local land that has fallen into neglect.

Cyclicity

One of the great gifts of nature is a knowledge of cyclicity. Our concept of 'linear time' is alienating and frightening, for it implies that things are finite and induces in us a sense of urgency and tension. Of course, it is necessary to face endings, and nature is a fine teacher in that respect each winter. However, all that dies is reborn, and a sense of cycle is another way to attune to the eternal, to the ever-renewing, ever-changing – and yet change*less* – aspect of creation. A cycle is like a spiral that we may travel, experience repeating yet deepening, taking us to deeper and higher levels of consciousness with each curve.

We have already encountered the Wheel of the Year in the shape of the eight festivals of Samhain, Yule, Imbolc, Spring Equinox, Beltane, Midsummer, Lughnasadh and Autumn Equinox. These are stages along the cycle where we take time to observe, celebrate and reorientate ourselves. These are explored in detail in *The Wheel of the Year – Myth and Magic Through the Seasons* (see Further Reading). One of the most potent forms of marking the festivals is by contact with the natural world, visiting, going for walks and generally observing the season. Different sites suggest themselves at different times of the year: the eerie Neolithic barrow clothed in Samhain mists; the solitary standing stone glistening with quartz as the ground glistens with frost at Yule; a garden of snowdrops or a holy well at Imbolc; a spring

meadow at the Spring Equinox; a glade with hawthorns at Beltane; a hilltop for Midsummer sunrise; a cornfield near such a place as Silbury Hill at Lughnasadh; an arboretum at the Autumn Equinox, in the glory of the year's flaming pyre. You can choose your own, where it feels right to you. Kathy Jones, in *The Ancient British Goddess* (see Further Reading) makes some interesting suggestions for places to visit at festivals, principally for those in the south-west of England. However, by entering into the spirit of the time of year, and of the land, you can find your own, whatever part of world you inhabit.

When we visit special places, whether this is a crop circle, standing stone or clump of trees, it should be in an attitude of pilgrimage, for how we approach the place will affect what it yields to us. If we come as tourists or for fresh air, we are likely to receive on that level, nothing more. Of course, the land belongs to us all, and we do not have to be mealy-mouthed or pious. However, in these overpopulated days it is as well to be considerate, and to give others the opportunity of experiencing the site in the way they wish. For instance, on a recent visit to West Kennet Long Barrow in the Avebury complex I really felt, for me, that it hadn't been worth the walk. It wasn't that remnants of rituals and spells and symbols chalked on the stone inside the barrow put me off – it was the cluster of pagans with their pentagrams and dangling ankhs on top of the barrow. These people were picnicking noisily and shouting at their toddlers. There are ways of creating an atmosphere of welcome and 'space' for others also, and this is an important part of respect for our world, enabling others to share and appreciate and heightening the consciousness of all concerned.

FINDING A SITE

If you have never found a place that is special to you, probably your first task is to affirm to yourself, strongly and clearly, that is what you want. It is rarely a good idea to go out and look, consciously, because that has a way of ensuring that you find a clump of nettles! (However, nettles may be growing on just the point of power one seeks!) You may like to look at a map of your locality and just let your mind wander, in the first instance, to any point of interest.

Sometimes there may be a name that catches your fancy, but that is more likely to be a blind alley. Just follow your nose and enjoy the exploration, without being gripped by the urgency to get a result. Philip Heselton, in *Secret Places of the Goddess* (see Further Reading) speaks of 'dowsing with the feet' to describe the process of letting your feet find that special place.

When you do find a place that feels good to you, give yourself the time to make contact. Try to sit without really thinking, and just observe. Don't look for extraordinary experiences. Take in the contours of the land and sky, leaves, tree-trunks, the movements of animals. Listen to all the sounds – sounds are easy to miss for there is usually the hum of a distant aeroplane or tractor that obliterates the closer, softer noises of small animals, plant growth and shifting soil. Notice smell especially, for that will speak to your instincts more surely than the other senses. Touch and feel, gently and with concentration. Then simply sit again, just 'being'. This is a most relaxing thing to do, and at the very least you will feel renewed and refreshed. It is an important part of getting to know *your* place, as it is for you.

All these activities have many functions. They can afford us simple pleasure, inspiration, relaxation, change of consciousness and widening of perspective. Really they are arguably the most important aspect of earth mysteries' exploration, for the earth is here, for us, and her mystery is ever laid out before us, and ever elusive. This is our personal response, having little to do with history, science or any other formal study and requiring only our participation to be real. Contact with the earth is about learning her languages – we cannot 'solve' earth mysteries with our modern, analytical means. As we have seen, there are many approaches to decoding the messages of the earth and the ancients who trod her, worshipped her and sculpted her. However, we can never truly understand the enigma unless we change our consciousness, too, quite radically, to retrieve the outlook of Stone Age humans and enter their world, which was that of an in-dwelling in nature itself. Our way to this, and possibly the only way, is by following the land into her own heart and into ours. Nature is the temple.

PRACTICE

In this chapter we have already encountered several things to do. In particular we have spoken of finding a special place and making a connection with it – and about all the activities you may want to carry out at this place.

Another activity you may like to try is psychometry. This involves putting yourself in a state of light trance, which just means a dreamy, receptive mode. It is best if you can feel secure and uninterrupted. If you are within easy travelling distance of a sacred site, place your hands upon a standing stone, or upon the contours of a barrow or the stones near a sacred well. Alternatively, visit your special place and place your hands upon the earth. What thoughts, feelings and impressions come to you? Do you see pictures in your mind? What images arise? Whatever they are, do not reason them away: take note, for they may have a special significance. You may be getting in contact with what has happened earlier at that place, or you may be formulating impressions that are important for you. It is best not to do this for too long, or you can become spaced out. You can always come back later on and try again, if you wish.

In addition, you may decide to undertake a variety of artistic, devotional or practical activities, or you may like simply to sit and tell yourself a story. Storymaking and storytelling are ancient and largely forgotten arts. Often a place will, by its very nature, give rise to a story. Let it speak through you.

Where you make contact with the earth is where you are in the presence of the mystery. Essentially, this is about experiencing, not thinking. It is a way of joy and wholeness, within ourselves and with our planet. Let it enrich your life.

FURTHER READING

I am particularly indebted to the following for information.

Earth Mysteries by Michael Howard (Hale, 1990). A 'magical mystery tour of our ancient past. Interesting and readable.

Earth Memory (Quantum, 1991), *Shamanism and The Mystery Lines* (Quantum, 1992), *Symbolic Landscapes* (Gothic Image, 1992) and *The New Ley Hunter's Guide* (Gothic Image, 1994), by Paul Devereux. Readers wishing for more information on the 'spirit flight' theory of ley lines will find this in *Shamanism and The Mystery Lines*, while *The Ley Hunter's Guide* is an excellent practical work on ley hunting.

Elements of Earth Mysteries by Philip Heselton (Element, 1991). A comprehensive, interesting and balanced overview by this author who has been involved for many years in the field of earth mysteries.

Needles of Stone Revisited by Tom Graves (Gothic Image, 1986). 'Magical technology' explained by dowser, Tom Graves.

Other Recommended Works

The Ancient British Goddess (Ariadne, 1991) and *The Goddess in Glastonbury* (Ariadne, 1996) by Kathy Jones.

The Ancient Science of Geomancy by Nigel Pennick (Thames & Hudson, 1979).

Circular Evidence by Pat Delgado and Colin Andrews (Bloomsbury, 1990). Best-selling account of crop circles.

Dictionary of Earth Mysteries (Thorson's, 1996), *The Secret Country* (Book Club Associates, 1976) and *Mysterious Britain* (Paladin, 1976), by Janet and Colin Bord. These authors are well known for their works about ancient sites in Britain.

Megaliths, Myths and Men by Peter Lancaster Brown (Book Club Associates, 1977). An introduction to astro-archaeology.

The Power of Limits by György Doczi (Shambhala, 1994). For those interested in the geometric elements of form.

Pyramid Power by Max Toth and Greg Nielson (Aquarian, 1988). All about pyramids.

The Old Straight Track (Abacus, 1974), *The Ley Hunter's Manual* (Turnstone, 1993), by Alfred Watkins. Seminal works.

Secret Places of the Goddess (Capall Bann, 1995) by Philip Heselton. This is a beautiful book about how and where to discover the Earth Spirit and to evoke pagan experience.

The Wheel of the Year – Myth and Magic Through the Seasons (Hodder & Stoughton, 1997) by Teresa Moorey and Jane Brideson. Customs and mythology surrounding the seasonal festivals, with crafts and suggestions of how to celebrate.

Amateur Astronomy and Earth Sciences magazine. Monthly publication, available from newsagents in the UK, and from Top Events Ltd, PO Box 1008, Chester CH3 9AE, UK. Tel: (44)1829 770884; Fax: (44)1829 771258.

The Ley Hunter. Editorial address: PO Box 258, Cheltenham, Glos. GL53 0HR, UK. Fax: (44)1242 224606; e-mail danny@thebureau.co.uk
US office: B & S (USA) Dept. TLH, Box 940, Beacon NY12508, USA Tel/fax: (914) 838 4340; e-mail leyhunt@aol.com

Publications by Robin Heath
A Key to Stonehenge, Bluestone Press, ISBN 0 952 6151-1-8
Sky Henge – the Alignment of Cosmos and Culture, Bluestone Press – to be published mid-1998.

Bluestone Press can be contacted at: Mags Yr Awel, Cwm Degwel, St. Dogmaels, Cardigan SA43 3JF, UK. Robin Heath can be e-mailed on: astrological.journal@zetnet.co.uk